INSIDE THE PRESIDENTIAL
PRESSURE-COOKER:
THE WHITE HOUSE MYSTIQUE

". . . The White House triggered in me the most profound religious experience of my life.

". . . The spiritual impact of the White House on the people who serve there is at the center of Watergate, and if this is not realized, we are doomed to repeat Watergates eternally.

"I was vulnerable to the distortions of power . . . And I was a Christian when I was being bent. How does a Christian yield to the temptations of power? That's what this book is all about."

—Wallace Henley

THE
WHITE HOUSE
MYSTIQUE

Wallace Henley

PILLAR BOOKS   NEW YORK

Unless otherwise identified, all Scripture quotations in this volume are from the King James Version of the Bible.

Scripture quotations identified NEB are from The New English Bible. © The Delegates of the Oxford University Press and the Syndics of the Cambridge University Press, 1961 and 1970. Reprinted by permission.

THE WHITE HOUSE MYSTIQUE

A PILLAR BOOK
Published by arrangement with Fleming H. Revell Company

Pillar Books edition published January 1977

ISBN: 0-89129-253-5

Library of Congress Catalog Card Number: 75-30774

Copyright © 1976 by Fleming H. Revell Company

Printed in the United States of America

PILLAR BOOKS
Pyramid Publications
(Harcourt Brace Jovanovich, Inc.)
757 Third Avenue
New York, New York 10017
U.S.A.

TO Lauri and Travis

Contents

Preface

Extracting oneself from the vortex of a tornado is a painfully bloody business. Yet this was the way I felt for months after leaving the White House. This book, perhaps, is a necessary part of that extraction for me personally.

And yet it is much more than that. Volumes have been written about the impact of the White House on senior-level officials, and their role in it. But someone—somewhere—must talk about the devastating emotional and spiritual impact of the place upon the junior-level staffer. For he is the faceless person who turns the screws and sharpens the axes at the behest of his master—the senior aide. And there is abundant evidence to suggest that Watergate—in the beginning and operational stages anyway—was the doing of some who had been junior-level staff members. Chronicles could doubtless be written about the mistakes of government wrought on this subtle, unseen level. So I have endeavored to write this book from that perspective.

This is a religious book, not because I wanted to set forth theology. It is a religious book of necessity, for the White House triggered in me the most profound religious experience of my life.

The book is critical, but not from a spirit of disrespect for institutions of government. It is not a Watergate book. With the rest of the nation, I have been pained over the political tragedy that unfolded in its wake—except I have the added burden of having served in the White House during that period. Further, I contributed to and was affected by the Watergate mentality attitudinally though not criminally.

My first book *Enter at Your Own Risk* was really an exploration into gaps I found in my own discipleship. It was completed the summer after I left the White House. Throughout that period, I searched for the spiritual threads that wove themselves into the tangled skein of Watergate. And somewhere along the way, I realized that Watergate, at its essence, was not made up of the overt things sticking out in congressional hearings and legal briefs, but in those subtle factors of humanity. To deal only with the legal aspects is to merely touch the surface. The spiritual impact of the White House on the people who serve there is at the center of Watergate, and if this is not realized, we are doomed to repeat Watergates eternally.

This book should not be read as a generalization. There are those who serve in places of high power who are not bent out of shape in the way I describe here. While the attitudes outlined in this book show up throughout Washington, and, indeed, throughout institutional life, they do not characterize everyone.

Maybe I risk my own image by discussing my personal vulnerability to the White House *milieu*. Yet I am compelled to share how the White House *mystique* worked on one young man, and to detail something of his attempt to wrench loose from it.

This is a book of optimism. I believe deeply in the Christian dialectic: Resurrection is always preceded by crucifixion. Resurrection is something reserved for people, but institutions can be resurrected through the human beings who make them up. Our political system has been crucified through the Watergate. But the introspection, the hunger for reform it has sparked can be redemptive. But it will *not* be, if legislation and nobler rhetoric are the only changes. The most urgent requirement is a change in the human spirit. Without apology, I am convinced more than ever that the change needed is the one brought about through a genuine encounter with Christ.

This is not cultural religion. That we had all through the Watergate days. In fact, I'm convinced that White House religion provided the philosophical backdrop against which political crimes were raised. No, the religious experience needed is that personal, life-shattering, but life-uniting existential encounter with Christ. It is the style I sought to outline in *Enter at Your Own Risk*.

I certainly do not hold that Christians should be the only people allowed in government. In fact, there are many Christians who don't belong there. But there must be in the spirit of the power-holder a commitment to a law and ethic transcending the expediencies he or she is up against daily. For me, there is no better statement of such high morality as that put forth by Jesus of Nazareth!

But I have already conceded I was vulnerable to the distortions of power, haven't I? And I was a Christian when I was being bent. How does a Christian yield to the temptations of power? That's what this book is about.

My debts of gratitude toward the many people who contributed—sometimes unwittingly—to this book are unpayable. I must start with my own family, who had to bear these struggles firsthand. The people of Old Spanish Fort Baptist Church took some admirable risks in accepting me as their pastor after I had been out of a church-related vocation an entire decade. Dr. Hudson Baggett and Jack Brymer of the *Alabama Baptist* have my deepest thanks for encouraging me to develop a White House series for publication in their paper. This book grew out of that series. I am also grateful to W. C. Fields and Bob O'Brien of Baptist Press (Southern Baptist Convention) for giving that series-wide exposure. Dick Ostling of *Time* magazine helped me more than he will know in pulling together my thoughts, as did Cal Thomas of KPRC-TV, Houston. Rev. Bob Curlee made a magnificent spiritual contribution that went into the very fabric of this book. I owe an especial debt of gratitude to Louis Moore, religion editor of the *Houston Chronicle,* who provided invaluable assistance in critiquing my work. I must say thanks to all the people who've sat through my lectures on the White House and Christian discipleship. Without the impetus of those speeches, I would have never been able to come to grips with all that happened to me while in Washington. My gratitude to Doug Coe, Louis Kramp, Dick Halverson, Fred Heyn, John Staggers and all the people who ministered to me through the Fellowship Foundation is unbounded! And finally, my special thanks to Chuck Colson who offered to write the Foreword that follows.

Foreword

Can man serve God and Caesar? Can he be obedient to Christ and the Commander-in-Chief as well? In *The White House Mystique* Wally Henley seeks an answer to this question of divided loyalties, which has plagued God's children for centuries.

Wally Henley, Baptist preacher turned writer, became an eager and ambitious White House aide during the Presidency of Richard Nixon. He paints a vivid portrait of the temptations and pressures swirling in the center of national power: flights on *Air Force One;* aides snapping salutes; sleek black limousines waiting; the dizzying whirl of parties and receptions; the sighs and roars of the crowds; the air charged with excitement and moments rich in history. The White House *mystique,* as Henley calls it, is a potent brew, intoxicating to a man's ambition, exhilarating to ego, and then destructive of his character. Henley examines with honesty how it nearly shattered his life.

Henley's White House experiences are entertaining and instructive as well. His philosophical observations about the moral distortions of the place upon the man (and vice versa) are perceptive and of enduring value to those who seek to study and understand the most important of the institutions of free society.

One might reasonably wonder how a junior staffer could provide insights not found in the books by the better-known employees of the White House—people who served Presidents—people like George Reedy, Bill Moyers, or Arthur Schlesinger. The answer to that is that such senior men must rely on the juniors to implement their policy decisions; hence, the young turks—or "young tigers" as they perhaps have been more aptly labeled—wield much greater power than the general public suspects. Then, too, of all the recent books and accounts of the White House and Watergate, this may be the first told from the exposed underside looking up. Henley has wiped the stardust from his eyes and provided a refreshing and revealing glimpse of the inner workings of the Presidency during this convulsive yet fascinating period.

During my experience in the White House as Special Counsel to the President, I remember Wally as one of the shavetails. But today Henley is quite another person—a brother in Christ—who ministered to me while I was in prison denims—and while the President we both served was being banished to political exile. White House protocol and man's lust for power once kept us far apart, yet we know today the closest of all bonds—and a Power in life far deeper and greater than anything we found in all of Washington's vast acres of granite and marble—its armies of bureaucrats—rows of stately embassies and near-regal trappings.

And in that lies an answer to life's confusion, which you will discover as you read *The White House Mystique.*

CHARLES W. COLSON

1

To Washington

The pundits were at their best on that hot July afternoon in 1970. But as an editor for the Birmingham *News,* I had scribbled through so many columns by Buckley, Kilpatrick, Evans and Novak, the Alsops, that the words meant to excite, reveal, shock, blurred into soft lullaby. Joseph Kraft disappeared under the fierce eye of my blue pencil and emerged as Brahms. I fought dozing at my desk. I couldn't know that within thirty minutes a telephone call would shatter through the dull afternoon and cast me into the Washington political caldron the columnists were writing about.

By the time the shrill ring roused my fading psyche, I had edited through enough "revelations" that I scarcely would have shuddered had it been told that Claire Booth Luce had once had a crush on Mao Tse-tung. All the monumental frets the columnists wrote about seemed to me the concerns of another universe.

Then the telephone call. I was surprised to hear the voice of Dr. Richard S. Brannon. A decade past, he had been my wife's pastor, prior to our marriage. I had since read that Brannon had gone to work in Washington, at the Office of Economic Opportunity.

His governmental career had been helped along by a high Presidential aide named Harry Dent, who had been a deacon in a church Brannon once pastored in South Carolina. Dent, though I couldn't know it at the time, would play an important role in my life over the ensuing three years.

Brannon told me he had been detailed temporarily to a unit known as the Cabinet Committee on Education. The group had been established by President Nixon to rally federal resources to aid desegregating school districts. Vice-President Spiro Agnew was the chairman. The Cabinet Committee, said Brannon, needed a press man who had worked in the South. He wanted to know if I were interested.

Affirmatives rolled off my tongue like liberated canaries. I had fantasized often about Washington, but I never dreamed the day might come when I would see the fantasies given a chance to become reality. Now that was staring me in the face!

There was only one hitch, continued Brannon. The Cabinet Committee wanted to move fast. I would have to be in Washington the next day. As soon as I hung up, I began arranging the trip. Few men have been blessed with a more supportive wife than mine. In the 1964 Presidential election, Irene had planned to write in my name until she discovered I was under age. Her one-woman boomlet for HENLEY FOR PRESIDENT tuckered out, but never her encouragement for me to chase the dreams we both thought were the foundation of our lives. I didn't have to convince her I should go to Washington and check out the job offer.

Once before, I had seen her help sell every parcel of furniture we possessed so we could move to Germany, and the pastorate of a small congregation in Nuremberg. Despite a real struggle there, the flicker of adventure and the romantic life was growing into flame. If this worked out, I told myself, it wouldn't be another Germany. I would do that for Irene, if for no other reason. Ironically, it would be Irene who would have to bear additional burdens because of the decisions I would make in months to come.

Throughout the day in Washington, I tried to look as erudite as possible. I wanted to make sure no one discovered my only previous visit had been during a stay with a Virginia cousin.

The offices of the Cabinet Committee hummed with what seemed its own life-force. Once I plucked from the sea a wooden plank covered with miniscule marine animals. The whole board vibrated with life as if the strum of eating and mating and dying were intrinsic to the wood itself. Without knowing it, at the Cabinet Committee that day, I was already succumbing to a dangerous mystique enveloping institutions of great power—a mystique having a devastating warp effect on the novice. To me, the pulse at the Cabinet Committee was as quick and valid as that of the sea animals on the plank of wood.

Robert C. Mardian, executive director of the Cabinet Committee, hurriedly shook my hand, as he mumbled something about finishing a report for the President. *The President?* my mind seemed to shout back. It was beginning to occur to me that the President did exist, that he was not a mythical creature roaming the halls of the White House like some frustrated minotaur. As Mardian pumped my hand, telephone consoles blinked on and off. To me, they were mystery boxes, their wires leading to other mystery boxes on the desks of very important people, who previously lived only in the newspaper columns I edited.

Well-starched, hyperserious young aides scurried about, until someone corralled several of them, who were introduced to me. One of the aides took my particulars, and told me they would call me in Birmingham in a few days.

Exactly one day later, I heard from Mardian's executive assistant. He was offering me the position of assistant director of the Cabinet Committee on Education, at a salary of nearly twenty thousand dollars a year. To an ambition-laden greenhorn proud because he was pressing toward ten thousand dollars a year, the offer was mind-boggling. Visions raced through my skull. I was rushing in with profound solutions to previously grueling bureaucratic mysteries, spilling my wisdom to Spiro Agnew, or John Mitchell, or Elliott Richardson, or—did I dare hope—President Nixon himself. I would be *Superaide!*

The assistant told me Mardian wanted me on the job in one week. That seemed unreasonable and impossible. I didn't understand at the time that quarters of Washington—particularly the White House—found suspect anything not unreasonable and impossible. Nevertheless, I agreed to be on the job in one week. My Washington career was not going to be impaled on the calendar.

Irene and I agreed I would move on to Washington, while she stayed in Birmingham long enough to sell the house. I fretted an entire day over how to break the news to my bosses at the newspaper, since they had every right to expect at least two weeks' notice. At last I scrounged up enough courage to present the case to Vincent Townsend, Sr., vice-president of the Birmingham *News*. Additionally, Mardian called Townsend and said great things about how urgently I was needed in Washington. That increased my already-inflated sense of importance. Much later I would wonder why the Cabinet Committee had waited so long to hire an information officer, and then rush with the fury of a scalded banshee to get him on the job. Townsend was most generous. He turned me loose and even offered me a leave of absence for a year so I sould take the job. I rejected that offer, saying I wanted to be "open-ended" in Washington. Already I decided I would angle for a permanent spot on the White House staff.

On August 10, 1970, I began my Washington sojourn. The first day was exciting enough. I was dispatched to the White House press room to meet Ron Ziegler's staff. My press releases would be coordinated through them. I lingered in the press room for the afternoon briefing, taking in sights and sounds from another world.

Mundane things, however, kept crushing in on me, reminding me I was very much a stranger on that new planet. From Ziegler's office, I went to my telephone and a marathon attempt to discover from the transit company information office which bus I should take out to Virginia, where I was staying. Black limousines darted through the streets. I joined the hassle on K Street for the Fairfax bus. I kept telling myself this would not last long.

Washington gave me one of its surprising baptisms during my first week on the job. Throughout the week, several of my colleagues on the Cabinet Committee staff seemed to have disappeared. Late in the week. I found it was because President Nixon was going to New Orleans to meet with private citizen groups which the Cabinet Committee staff had assembled. But no one told me anything about the trip.

On Friday, August 14, I arrived at the Cabinet Committee to find the doors locked tight. Inside, I could hear a telephone pleading to be answered, and I wrestled with my new set of keys. I caught the telephone just in time. A female voice asked, "Who's this?" I told her. The caller turned out to be Mardian's secretary. "You're supposed to be here in New Orleans," she said. President Nixon was to depart shortly, and I knew there was no way I could get to New Orleans in time for the meetings he was to conduct. But the secretary had an answer. "Stand by," she said. (I learned early that one stands by a lot in Washington.)

Moments later, the telephone jangled again. The secretary said she had called the White House motor pool, and a car was being dispatched to deliver me to Andrews Air Force Base, where I would board the White House backup plane. (Now the backup plane is not really that, in that it does not go behind the President, but before him. It carries staff and important personages who do not rate a ride on *Air Force One* on a given trip. In this case, the backup plane was carrying the domestic cabinet members who made up the Cabinet Committee. It was to be my first encounter with the Brahmins.)

The building in which the Cabinet Committee was headquartered had two doors—one in front and one in back. At my house, the front and back doors have the same address. I assumed the same principle would apply at our building. So when the White

House motor pool called, I told them my address, and went promptly to the front door. I had not learned the ways of Washington. The front-door address was not that of the back-door, and it was the address to that entrance I had given the motor pool. The car came, waited, and left—without me. The minutes were ebbing by. Finally, it was only a half hour until departure of the backup plane, and I knew it took that long to get to Andrews. At that moment, the Cabinet Committee's driver came walking up. I snared him, told him the situation and within minutes, we were off.

We screeched into Andrews just as the Gargantuan airplane was reaching the end of the taxiway. The engines idled as the pilots went through their checklists. I dashed into the waiting area, and told the officer on duty I had to get on the jet. My name had by then been added to the manifest. However, said the duty officer, whether to abort the takeoff and take me aboard would have to be the pilot's decision. Just to be sure no time was wasted, he had me ride in a jeep to the runway near the idling plane, as the control tower relayed the message to the pilot.

The noise from the engines threatened the health of our ears, but we finally got the green light. We crawled nearer the massive plane. No engines were silenced, no doors opened, until a tiny hole appeared in the floor of the cockpit, which now was several feet above my head. An air-force steward descended on a rope ladder, and beckoned me to follow him back up.

By now, the airplane had been sitting on the end of the runway some twenty minutes. It had no windows in the passenger compartment. In short, it was not the place to do a lot of waiting. The Attorney General of the United States, the Secretary of Health, Education and Welfare, the Postmaster General, the Secretary of Housing and Urban Development, Counselors to the President and assorted courtiers glared at me as I stumbled to the rear compartment reserved for the lowest of aides—who, by the way, still out-ranked me, since I was to have flown to New Orleans on a commercial flight in the first place.

At any rate, I was now formally introduced to Washington.

I met President Nixon during my second week in Washington. One of the newly formed citizen groups for public education had come to town for its introduction to the President. Mardian always saw to it his assistant directors had to be present for the formal meetings in the Oval Office. For a man not famous for his mellow demeanor, it was a nice deed.

Charles de Gaulle, in his memoirs, wrote: "All my life, I have thought of France in a certain way . . . like the princess in the fairy story or the Madonna in the frescoes, as dedicated to an exalted and exceptional destiny" (cited in Aidan Crawley's *de Gaulle*). My preconceptions of the Presidency were as idealized as were de Gaulle's thoughts about France. The Oval Office was the inner sanctum of the Temple of the Presidency. Now as I stood in the Roosevelt Room, just across from the Oval Office, it struck me I was about to enter the Realm itself. Beyond the sturdy white door presided over by a dour-faced Secret Service agent, Kennedy had rocked himself into immortality, Eisenhower had daddied a frightened Cold War America and FDR had cooked up his magic elixir for the treatment of limpid nations. I was really hooked on the mystique of the Presidency.

My turn came to meet the President, and Mardian introduced us. Nixon recalled that Clarence Hanson, publisher of the Birmingham *News,* owned stock in a soft-drink company, and had once asked lawyer Nixon to represent the firm. We talked about the fine points of the soft drink, how nice it was for a young journalist to be where I was, and that was the sum total of my conversation with the President of the United States. The White House tapes doubtlessly have enscribed the discussion for posterity.

Inspired by the encounter with the Boss, I plunged into the work of the Cabinet Committee. I was assigned to write a history of the group, and in a single weekend, I cranked out a two-hundred-page dissertation. Somebody felt it was important enough to order the officers on the Cabinet Committee to submit to an interview with me. But nothing was ever done with the history. Though it began almost frenetically, it was as soon forgotten as if the assignment had never been made.

Undaunted, I charged on. I spent Labor Day weekend 1970 in a television studio in Charlotte, North Carolina, editing videotapes of Billy Graham urging people to support public education.

By the time of the second trip planned for the Cabinet Committee, I planned to be ready. (I wouldn't miss my airplane this time!) The journey would take the Cabinet officers to Atlanta for an update meeting with the citizen groups. Weeks in advance, I had alerted the White House press office to the trip. My understanding was that they would notify the Atlanta press that nearly half the President's

Cabinet would visit their city, and I would handle on-site press matters.

I arrived in Atlanta Friday evening, hoping to get some rest before arrival of the Cabinet members the following morning. I decided, however, I should check in with the major press people and let them know I was in town. One by one as I phoned newspapers and television stations, it was apparent they had not been told the dignitaries were visiting their city. Several of the press folk were livid. I called the White House, and could find no one available to tell me what to do. I sat on my bed pondering the sad start we were off to with this trip.

The telephone rang again. It was one of my superiors from Washington. Not only would I handle the press, he said, but I would be in charge of getting the Cabinet officers from the airport to the hotel, and of mapping out their movements to the various meeting rooms. I had no idea how I would be available to assist the press, and at the same time play Indian guide for the Cabinet officers. But I knew I would try.

To make the affair really interesting, a convention of photographers were being held at the hotel. They filled the cavernous lobbies of the place, and I got frightful little visions of Cabinet members being nipped off from the group and surrounded by popping flash bulbs. So, I discovered a back corridor leading from the suite where we would place the Cabinet members on arrival, to their first meeting room. The transfer went smoothly. However, when the press found the Cabinet officers had come in the back door, they concluded the officials had secrets to hide and were seeking to avoid the press. Since I was then doing my Indian guide routine with the Cabinet, I wasn't available to clarify things for the newspeople. Media-wise, the thing was sad. But now I was catching on to the ways of Washington bureaucracy. A cold fatalism was settling over me as well. I knew I had tried desperately to keep all the bits and pieces juggling on the Atlanta trip, but it appeared as a failure anyway. Later, I would hear a White House wag say that if one of us were to walk on water, it would be reported like this:

A White House aide walked on water today. However . . . .

This fatalism was devastating. Frustrated, weary, it was too easy to conclude that trying sometimes was not worth the effort, since no matter how great the success, someone would make it appear as the most colossal of failures.

Following the school openings of 1970, Mardian was assigned as assistant-attorney general over the Internal Security Division of the Department of Justice. He was asking his special assistants at the Cabinet Committee to move with him. But that one clearly was not for me, I concluded. I had not even known there was an Internal Security Division, let alone what it did. Besides, the White House was my goal, not the Justice Department.

But after a few weeks of this attempted turnoff, an aide to Mardian gently gave me the word: "You don't have a lot of choice in the matter. You are being detailed to the Justice Department."

The irony was immense. Attorney General Mitchell had ordered Mardian to beef up the Internal Security Division, so I heard, to help deal with domestic unrest. Mardian placed me in charge of public affairs, where I felt at home. That job consisted largely of answering thousands of pieces of mail coming to the President, J. Edgar Hoover, and Mitchell, regarding allegedly subversive groups. Usually, all I had to do was select the proper computer program, since most of the replies were handled by machine. But I had also been asked to oversee Congressional relations for the Internal Security Division. I did not feel at home in that post, since I had never had experience with the Congress. Sometimes in Washington the most maximally unqualified person winds up with the job.

This assignment at Justice held for four very difficult months. I realized I could take no more, and faced the fact that my alternative was to resign from the government. I prepared a letter, and presented it to Mardian. (One of my most vivid memories is that of one of his secretaries telling me what a shame it was I would have to miss the 1972 campaign.)

I told Richard Brannon what I was doing, and he offered to get me a job at the Office of Economic Opportunity. But I was tired of being shunted from place to place, especially into jobs I had no qualifications to hold. Anyway, the White House seemed beyond my grasp.

Then one day, Brannon called again. His former parishioner, Harry Dent, the Presidential Special Counsel, wanted to have lunch with me at the White House. There might be some talk about a job, said Brannon. The three of us met in Dent's Executive Office Building suite and walked across West Executive Avenue to the West Wing, and the dining room.

As we entered the small "mess room" (I put the words in quotes because it seems incongruent to call such an elegant place a "mess"), I spotted men whose names I once helped spell correctly and get properly capitalized in the columns I edited for the *News*. I was surrounded by the people who were said to run the country. Then Dent got down to business: "I'd like you to join my staff here in the White House." The word *no* was as foreign to me as ancient Sanskrit. I was Robinson Crusoe being asked if he'd like to come home!

Months later, I would try to analyze my compulsion to work in the White House, to view it, during those Washington years as almost *raison d'être*. There was, of course, the easily decipherable. I believed firmly in the ideals the Nixon administration was articulating in 1969 and 1970. The New Federalism, implemented by revenue sharing, would restore a new power balance to states and localities. Welfare reform, in the pattern I heard the administration proposing it then, seemed to me a realistic way of assaulting poverty. In short, I perceived in 1970 a President Nixon who had a realistic fix on the future without compromising the promise of the future.

And then there were the notions about a so-called secular ministry. At age fifteen, God had called me in unmistakable terms: to minister. I had majored in Bible in college, and gone directly to seminary without the slightest hesitation. But by the midsixties, I was rethinking the whole course of my life. Hard experiences in some churches played a minor role in sparking this reassessment. But the ideological contortions of the period was beginning to twist me.

My own interpretation—or misinterpretation, as the case may be—of two of my theological heroes of the era was bending and stretching me into a rubber-band religion. Harvey Cox's ideas about secularity colored my views of the ministry in those days. The emphasis more and more was on the "irrelevancy" of the church, and the "uselessness" of the pastoral ministry. In my intellectual circles then it was seen as a good way to waste a life. The pop philosophy of the day said that the preaching ministry wasn't where the action was. And, watching white churches struggle with the race question seemed to me a test of the validity of the contention that the church was an institution more concerned with its own survival than with being prophetic with the Truth. Former Bishop James Pike, whom I had interviewed, had doffed his collar and was forming a church alumnus group; herds of ministers were getting into new psychological techniques; and the Office of Economic Opportunity (OEO) was referred to facetiously as the "Office of Ecclesiastical Opportunity" because so many ex-clerics were populating its employment rolls.

Sadly, I found myself losing the driving zeal to become a pastor. I was becoming increasingly disoriented, struggling to maintain identity, direction, purpose. I had thought of nothing but being a preacher for more than a decade, and had spent all my energies equipping myself for that work. Now, I realized, I would have to find something else to do.

But I clung to the desire to minister. It was at this point that my other "hero" provided the theological backdrop against which I would move during that period. Paul Tillich's ideas had enamored me. He talked of faith as something philosophical, and he stressed the need of moving theological talk into the philosophical sphere. Jesus became for me an abstraction, part of the nebulous mass known as the "Ground of all being." He was no longer the Suffering Servant who had grueling contact with people in the despairing wildernesses and villages of Galilee. He was more an idea than a reality for me at that time. Nor was He a Person who retreated to mountains for long prayer sessions with the Father. That phenomenon belonged to the pietists, and I was bent on being a secularist!

Thus, when the White House offer came, I could think of no better forum for the exercise of my so-called secular ministry, buoyed up by my abstract, philosophical, non-experiential theological nonsystem. I was shelving many of the firm convictions that had anchored and stabilized my earlier life. I couldn't know it then, but going into the White House without a granitelike set of convictions was like sailing into a hurricane without a rudder!

Psychologically, I was ripe for the White House invitation, too. My father, for whom I am named, was an alcoholic. In his later years, it was particularly messy. He was a tragic figure groping across the lives of his family. I wanted desperately to reach back in love. But the alcohol always distorted our attempts to reach each other. I felt rejected by him, and I am sure he felt rejected by me.

He and my mother were divorced, but he lived nearby. Many nights, in a drunken rage, he would come to our house, beating on doors and windows while we crouched in terror in the corner. Usually, the only respite was after we had summoned the police, and the squad car had carried him off. The shame was intense, and without knowing it, I was developing severe image hang-ups.

A hunger for prestige and recognition was growing in me. It was a substitute for the attention I craved, as a child, from him. By 1971, I thought I was over the tragedy of my father, who had died in 1966. But by then, the hunger for acceptance had buried itself deep into my psyche, and I could not see on that day in the West Wing mess that the hunger for prestige and recognition was there as a remnant of the old days, helping propel my quick acceptance of Harry Dent's offer.

I would win admiration as a member of the White House staff, and this would help to clean up the name I bore—to give it honor. *Now* I understand that a major effort of my life up to that point had been to capture some dignity for the name.

So the White House job seemed to encompass everything I needed. I would be working for goals in which I beleived; I would have a "bully pulpit" for my secular ministry, and, because of the prestige and recognition, I would no longer have to struggle to exonerate my name!

2

The White House Warp

"Every time I leave this place, I feel like taking a bath."

The remark miffed me. The man was sitting in my office at the White House. He had been coming to the place for a decade or more, and I felt he should have known better. Now I understand. He *did* know. He had discovered what is most difficult to see when one is on the White House staff. He knew about the "White House Warp."

I had to get far away from 1600 Pennsylvania Avenue—in time and space—to really grasp the devastating impact of the White House Warp. Essentially, the Warp means that reality filters into the White House as through a prism. It is colored, distorted, bent as it flows from the day-by-day universe into a cosmos where the very vulnerable appears invulnerable and the mediocre superior. One seeking to deal with real-world problems doesn't always have a fix on things as they are, but as they appear.

Perhaps this was a reason Richard Nixon kept shoving the Watergate to the back burner until it showed him out of the White House. From the perspective of the Oval Office, there likely was a dizzying warped notion that the whole affair was no more than a troublesome gnat which would not dare light on the President of the United States.

Throughout the summer of 1972, after the bugging team had been caught at Democratic headquarters, memoranda and conversations flurried through the White House, urging the President—or someone—to seize the initiative in investigating and foraging up the truth. But such efforts kept bumping into that Warp, which by then was more like an invisible force field. The Watergate, went the notion, would disappear.

One suspects this was one of the ways Nixon was victimized himself by the White House. He may have helped intensify the Warp, but in the end, it slew him. I still remember a friend going to President Nixon, apologizing for a *faux pas* he had pulled in a press statement. Nixon's response, in effect, was for the man not to worry, that the public memory was short, and that within six or eight weeks, the boner would be forgotten. That was the Warp: Things would go away—not be bothersome.

"The fact remains," wrote George Reedy in *The Twilight of the Presidency,* "that the [White House] provides camouflage for all that is petty and nasty in human beings, and enables a clown or a knave to pose as Galahad and be treated with deference." The Warp thus affects people as well as issues. The lousiest of scoundrels, the most able liars—through the White House Warp—develop self-images of grandeur and honor, which they foist off on whoever will be gullible enough to take them. And the Warp affects public perceptions, so that there is a willingness to accept Barabbas as Galahad, simply because he occupies a desk in the White House!

As the Watergate became more and more a political apocalypse of horror, it was clear that in the short-term view, the United States was in for pain. In the long-term, however, I felt optimism. Perhaps the Watergate would be the shocking splash of cold water which would awaken Washington to the need of reforming the White House system, and examining general attitudes guiding our political system. The greatest hope would be that people in leadership would examine their own spirits, and that there would be a hungering for inner revolution—the kind wrought only by Christ. Schlesinger and other scholars of the Presidency suggest the White House passes through a trauma of corruption every half century or so, with a frightful regularity. But just maybe the extreme tragedy of Watergate will at least widen the cycle of a few decades.

The Warp itself is molded by the personality of a given administration. It manifests itself differently in a Nixon White House than it would, say, in an Eisenhower White House. A basic effect of the Warp on the White House of the early seventies was the appearance from within the White House of its being surrounded by "enemies" ready to attack at the drop of a syllable. We were gallant young men standing on the battlements, defending the perimeters of our lonely castle from the Huns who had it surrounded, and who were fed endlessly by their allies. And at the middle of the isolated castle was the one person for whom we fought—the President. His protection was the foremost—the only—priority of battle. The Huns, of course, were the political "enemies" someone in the White House had the poor judgment to catalog, and their resupplying allies were the media, academia, organized labor.

"One thing you should realize early on, we are practically an island here." Such was the warning issued a newcomer to the White House staff, Herbert Porter, by President Nixon's appointments secretary, Dwight Chapin (from an interview with Porter appearing in the *New York Times,* August 5, 1973).

I had never heard of an Enemies List until John W. Dean III disclosed its existence during the Senate Watergate hearings. But, remembering the fierce attitudes stirred by the Warp, I was not surprised to learn one had been drawn up. Obviously, every President, every leader has opponents, some of them drastic enough to be classed as *enemies.* But because of the Warp, circa 1969–1972, the seriousness, potency, and character of the so-called enemies were thrown into distortion. The opposition was not seen in balance.

There is, of course, a certain danger in talking of a White House Warp, as if human beings were impacted by some predetermined, irresistible force absolving them of responsibility. That would be a cop-out of the first magnitude. It is *people* who succumb to the Warp, and it is *people* who must bear the responsibility. It is not inevitable that everyone who works in the White House will have his actions and attitudes distorted by the Warp. But one has to be aware of it to resist it. Youth, naiveté, sheer selfishness can blind one to the Warp. But there is ample history to show that many White House aides have served admirably. They were the wise ones who saw the nature of things, and recognized what they should resist.

The political polarization in Washington during the first Nixon term fueled the Warp considerably. To a newcomer, the spirit of enmity was depressing. Coupled with the paranoia rampant in the Executive Branch at times was a politicized, distrustful Congress. When the two met, the clash was invariably bloody. It seemed no issue could be dealt with between the White House and Congress without an attempt being made by one or the other or both to politicize the matter, to squeeze from it every drop of political blood. The nation, of course, was the victim in the battle.

To us novices on the White House staff, watching the battle was an interesting spectator sport. There was, for example, that evening when Congressional Republicans were invited to the White House for photographs with the President. "Pete" McCloskey, the California Representative planning to challenge Nixon for the Presidential nomination, attended. As the Congressmen were herded into a receiving room for a handshake and photo with the President, some of us noted McCloskey joining the line. We hovered at the doorway, waiting for McCloskey and Nixon to be eyeball to eyeball. The moment came midst the nicest of greetings—to our surprise. In retrospect, I'm not sure what we expected. Perhaps McCloskey would spit in Nixon's eye. Maybe the President would refuse to shake his hand!

Which was another devastating result of the Warp: Barbarisms are always the work of the enemy. All that stands in the way of political reconciliation is for the other side to admit their error. When it came to political sin, the Warp always twisted the guilt to the other side.

Gradually, I became aware that there was an alternative to this immobilizing polarization. That alternative was expressed in the work of a group of people in Washington determined to introduce government leaders to the reconciling spirit of Chirst. The movement was committed to the idea that, through Christ, a new center could be found to bind together even the most rabid opponents. Experience had taught those in the Fellowship—as the movement was called—that love for Christ could transcend the things dividing people.

One day, Harry Dent invited me to meet with several White House staffers who were trying to get a prayer cell organized there. Three of us began meeting on a regular basis, and determined to try to enlarge the group. We soon developed an interest in reaching out to other prayer cells we heard existed on Capitol Hill and in several federal agencies. Doug Coe, a full-time worker with the Fellowship, attended some of our sessions. Gradually, we got to know participants in some of the other cells. They included some of our so-called enemies! Praying with them was a sobering experience. The White House group enlarged to about fifteen regulars, including (in late 1972) Egil Krogh, reputed chief of the so-called White House Plumbers.

By 1973, the prayer cell had opened White House doors which had been shut for a long time. For example, occasional attenders included Charles Colson and Senator Harold Hughes. There had been no greater Nixon partisan than Colson, and few who could have exceeded Hughes in their opposition to Nixon. Yet, by 1973, these men occasionally came to the White House staff prayer breakfast together.

Through the fellowship, and participation in the National Prayer Breakfast, I found myself trafficking quite heavily with the opposition. I met people in media, in the Judicial and Legislative Branches. And getting together to wrestle over common concerns in prayer seemed a vast improvement over that other reason-for-gathering—the Washington cocktail party.

The best hope for ending the bitter polarization bending the political system out of shape was the spirit of community, of familyhood, existing between men and women whose lives were committed to Christ. And it remains so now. The only other unifying factors in Washington political life are those of expediency, or ideology. Occasionally, an issue will arise capable of pulling together political enemies. But such unifiers are temporary, and what Washington needs is a constant. Christ is dynamic. He is alive in those who receive Him, through the Holy Spirit. The *last* thing Washington needs is another philosophy. Christ is the answer to political polarization because to be His disciple is to be indwelt with a life seeing itself as relational. Christ spurs a love that is to be nonexploitive, a love working only as it is shared, and that means between Republicans and Democrats, liberals and conservatives. Wherever the dynamic of the Living Christ has taken hold in Washington, there is beautiful oneness, even in passionate disagreement. I know because I've seen it!

But the White House Warp deepened the sensation of being surrounded to include not only those outside the administration, but to many within its very gates. To return to the analogy of the besieged castle: previously, the kingdom in which the castle sat had been occupied by so-called foreigners, who had left many of their own living covertly in the kingdom; now, these within the kingdom joined with the outsiders in the assault on the castle. We were thus surrounded from without and within, and the castle was indeed an island to itself.

Again, it goes without saying that a Presidency is going to have opposition, and, given Civil Service laws, some of that opposition will be from holdovers from previous administrations. There were frequent references in the White House to President Eisenhower's failure to make over the Executive Branch in a more Republican image during his two terms in the Presidency. A political party for Eisenhower had apparently been a vehicle for running for the Presidency, and there had been no fierce commitment to clean out Democrats in the Executive Branch. Consequently, went the argument, Presidents Kennedy and Johnson had a strong bureaucratic base on which to enlarge, and the Democratic hold on the machinery of the Executive Branch grew considerably. To the Republican White House, that meant policy ordered by the President might be sidetracked or derailed altogether at lower bureaucratic levels. One day, early in my Washington stay, I got a firsthand look at the intensity of these feelings. We had been conducting a meeting on school desegregation in the Roosevelt Room, across from the Oval Office. Part of the discussion had been over funding the President had ordered be made available to help desegregating school districts. An aide from the Department of Health, Education and Welfare was talking with a member of the staff of the Cabinet Committee on Education.

I caught the conversation just as my colleague

from the Cabinet Committee snarled, "Do you mean to tell me that the President of the United States cannot have funds he has ordered?" Apparently, the man from HEW was saying they might not agree to freeing the money.

Sometimes, the long-term strategy of the Nixon administration filtered down to my level. The plan, as I caught it, was for the President to build a broad base of support during the first term, so that he would have a genuine mandate in the second. Then, in that second term, the President would revolutionize the federal government with thoroughly Republican philosophies. Proponents of this theory of the Nixon Presidency said it explained his apparent lack of philosophical consistency during the first term.

To some (among them a few Nixon so-called friends) this deteriorated after Watergate to nothing more than a survival strategy. Howard Phillips, the outspoken conservative appointed by Nixon to dismantle the Office of Economic Opportunity, broke with the President over this issue. By 1974, Phillips was calling on conservatives to help remove Nixon from office, accusing Nixon of clinging to the survival strategy, which had displaced concern "for the long-range good of the nation with crass considerations of short-run political advantage."

Nevertheless, had the long-term plan been carried out, there likely would have been upheaval in the Executive Branch. Foreshadowings of this were given in the early days of the second term, as moves were under way to cut the White House staff. But suspicion ran deep, and the cuts would not have been limited to the President's immediate staff.

Thus, the White House Warp caused the place to

be a vat of seething mistrust. At times, some in the White House wondered if they could trust one another. To stand with some balance (under such distorting circumstances) takes the strongest of men. Unfortunately, the staffing process doesn't always take such subtle requirements in mind.

Which is why, perhaps, there was such a fixation in the White House on youth. One-third of the Nixon staff during the first term was thirty years old or younger. To be sure, this was positive politics, for America impaled itself happily on the Apollo complex. Even some of the senior aides to the President—like Ron Ziegler and John W. Dean III—were alumni of the Howdy Doody and Mickey Mouse Club generation. And where the senior aides were older people, many of their junior staffers were from the thirty-or-younger bracket. This meant the aides responsible for implementing decisions dwelt in the ranks of the inexperienced.

The White House Warp at this point was influenced by a larger, cultural warp. The myth had gone up and down the land that the current harvest of young adults was the most brilliant ever. Weekly—from pulpit and editorial page—went the vast generalization that this generation had important things to say, and that America had better listen.

It would be just as wrong to generalize the other way, and say that to be young is a curse of sorts. But it's just that in youth, the judgment and experience so desperately needed in White House jobs are sadly lacking. George Reedy said that no one should serve at the White House until he is at least forty years old and suffered one major disappointment in life. As one who joined the staff at twenty-nine, I must agree with Reedy.

The impact of the White House Warp on the young can have disastrous consequences. Reedy, again, calls the effect demoralizing on the young. The headiness of being there throws everything out of balance. There was a certain thrill to ordering up a car from the White House motor pool, and have a military driver snap at your order. During my time in the White House, I traveled frequently on speaking assignments. I never tired of the airport welcome, of television cameras and reporters probing for my "wisdom" on this or that. Because of my youth—partly—these incidental factors became my real world, and subconsciously I determined to do nothing to end all that. It was too easy for morality and conscience to become subservient to the goal of maintaining the trimmings.

For one challenge facing the young aide immediately on arrival at the White House is the fact he must establish himself. The veteran politician or ment. The young aide is where he is because of an accident—of happening to be in the right place at the right time. And he has the staggering awareness that if he plays the game right, he will be elevated to senior statesmanship at a very young age.

The young aide, therefore, must be ever watchful for opportunities to show his proficiency. So a senior staffer muses about how nice it would be to know what Larry O'Brien is thinking these days, and the next step, conceivably, is that an overhearing junior aide is seeing to it that the boss, who owns all the lollipops, is getting that information.

Why was there such an interest in putting so many young people on the White House staff? Was it because our limited experience kept us from knowing the right questions to ask? Was it because we were more likely to be overwhelmed so that we could not challenge and debate and say the unpronounceable word (which is *no*)?

Another dilemma of the junior staff member is that he must be able to assume that the orders he is given from his superiors come from honorable intentions and needs and are legitimate. He is at the mercy of such an assumption, and nice young people have gone to jail because such assumptions were not valid.

Thus the Warp feeds on its own. It creates distortions, and as the distortions broaden, the Warp intensifies. And in the White House of the first Nixon term, the very vulnerable were there, volunteering to be gobbled up.

Anyone, however, who thinks the Warp departed the White House with Nixon is on shaky ground. True, he gave his own stamp to it. But it is peculiarly a child of our secular age, working its chaos on institutions of all sorts. One of the hoaxes of the secular city suggests that if we create an institution with worthy goals, the goodness of men will be amplified as they are collected under its roof. The truth is that institutions amplify opportunities for the corruption of power. So Reedy points out that "The factor that I have missed in most of the works on the presidency I have read is the impact of the institution on individuals. The literature on the subject seems to assume that the White House somehow molds the man and his assistants into finer forms. . . ."

Washington needs desperately to hear Saint Paul say: "All have sinned, and come short of the glory of God" (Romans 3:23). For the Warp works best where people blind themselves to their own vulnerability. Perhaps more than anything else, that is the meaning of the Warp: *blindness.*

3

Superaide

"This is the White House operator. Stand by please for a call from San Clemente." I was in Jackson, Mississippi, playing the friendly fed, setting up a press conference to announce awarding of a major grant to the city's school system. I couldn't imagine that anyone in San Clemente even knew of my existence, let alone where I was. But the White House operators are known for a mysterious omniscience capable of locating anybody, anywhere, at any time.

Soon Bob Mardian's voice came on the line. I had become acquainted with two levels of anger in Mardian. The first was in the class of an exploding atomic bomb. The second was a controlled slow stew. Mardian's voice was taut. I could tell by its sound his teeth were gritted. I readied for the lambast.

"I want to read you something," he said. The words had appeared earlier that day in the Los Angeles *Times*. My stomach dangled over a bottomless precipice of nausea as Mardian read. The day before, I had put together a press conference in Alabama, where then-Governor Albert Brewer had conferred with members of our federal advisory committee for the state. It had been my first assignment in the field. In fact, I had just made the move to Washington. I had not completed the metamorphosis from reporter to press agent.

A man from the *Times* had cornered me before the press conference, and began to ask me for background information. *I* would set a new pattern for relations between the administration and the press. *I* would be candid, open, especially if it were on a "deep background" basis. Washington would be amazed I had mastered the technique so early.

So I told the reporter the feeling existed that the advisory committees had been set up a bit late, since they were supposed to be working on school openings scarcely a month away. They would do a good job, anyway, I said, stressing it would have been much better to have had them circulating earlier.

As Mardian reread my words, there was little doubt about whose mouth they had darted from. The reporter did not name me, but he did attribute the remarks to the spokesman for the President's Cabinet Committee on Education. Other than Mardian, I was the only spokesman, and we both understood quite well that Mardian had not made such statements. Further, as I got it from Mardian, Nixon was at San Clemente, had read the story, and had called Mardian's attention to it. What an irony: I at last had gotten the President's attention!

I had barely gotten my feet on the ground in Washington, and it appeared my departure was already being plotted. From Jackson, I flew to New Orleans to make plane connections to Washington. In New Orleans, I called Irene. "Honey, I'm not sure you ought to unpack those boxes," I moaned. I explained to her what had happened, and with her typical disposition of iron, she laughed off the whole thing. I felt better. That was on Friday. We passed a pleasant—though tense—weekend.

On Monday morning, I boarded the Trailways bus which plowed through the torrent of traffic between Fairfax, Virginia, and Washington. The Lord be praised for lousy traffic and long bus rides, I thought, as I sorted through the various confrontations I might have to respond to on my arrival at the office. Once there, I scooted to my office, hoping to shut out the world. It would not be done. A secretary told me I had been summoned to the office of Ed Morgan, at the White House. Morgan was the official overseer of all utterances from the Cabinet Committee.

Morgan's office was really in the Executive Office Building, an annex of the White House. The EOB, as it was known in acronymic bureaucratese, was a monument to nineteenth-century architectural orgies. To me, it resembled one of those bleak old orphanages where children were beaten and left hungry. Funny, I thought, but an office in that building had been my target. Now I was probably on my way to execution.

It was stayed. Morgan gave me a mild upbraiding; I promised I would forever curb my tongue; and back across Pennsylvania Avenue I went, my fame and glory intact, and my future job still on the horizon, with only a modicum of gray here and there.

Somewhere, somehow, Andy Hardy had to grow up. David, killer of Goliath, had to cross over to David, conqueror of Bathsheba. Washington would not permit the perpetual naiveté and innocence of Little Orphan Annie. The close brush with extinction taught me I was now in a crass contest characterized by the survival of the fittest. *Fit* here meant being canny, wily, capable of sprouting a good line, and above all distrustful of everybody.

Upon my official entrance into the White House family, I realized that we were all expected to measure to myth. Conventional wisdom—the myth—was that the White House is filled with brilliant people roaming its caverns uttering profound thoughts. At least that was the myth prior to Watergate. It was an atmosphere of expectation into which I moved.

The truth is that the White House was crammed with people, a few of them even brilliant. Most often, however, it was not the pursuit of profundity that propelled us, but the chase for the White House version of the Holy Grail. To be crowned *Superaide* was the prize we sought. Superaide was the epitome of the faceless but faithful, upward-bounding, unquestioning servant of the awesomely placed people who ran the country. George Reedy's description of this pursuit as resembling a barnyard in which everyone is struggling for a better place in the pecking order is too mild. The contest I entered was more like a jousting match. Only we weren't striking blows for the approval of the charming princess, but for the nod of the king himself!

If Superaide was to be skeptical and distrustful of everyone, the blunder with the *Times* had certainly rooted those seeds. And an experience while working at the Justice Department Internal Security Division spurred in me the growth of this attitude to jungle proportions.

It was the last week of April 1971. Washington was getting ready for another anti-war marathon, only this one seemed more serious than the rest. The demonstrators were calling themselves Mayday People, and were saying their goal was to shut down the government. Cots were moved into our offices at the Justice Department. However, I was out of touch with much of the internal planning and worry, since my job was wrestling with bags of mail and telephone calls inundating us from Congress and public.

Two or three days before Mayday, Mardian summoned me to his office. Two youngsters from the Mayday camp had appeared in the office of a certain Senator, asking to talk with someone from the government. Mardian wanted me to go.

It might be asked here quite logically why I would be sent to debrief the demonstrators, and not a trained professional—say an FBI agent. Despite a public image to the contrary, the administration in those days wasn't all that high on J. Edgar Hoover. This bad blood carried over, tainting relations between the FBI and Internal Security Division. There were those in the Division who said that Hoover didn't really understand the nature of the modern anarchist. The irony was that while Hoover's understanding may have been limited, mine was almost nonexistent! Nevertheless I departed for Capitol Hill, after being told by a friend I would likely be fed false information to mislead the government, or kidnapped for hostage.

The boy and girl I met that day in the Senate Office Building seemed hardly capable of a kidnapping. They told me they had come to Washington full of idealism. They wanted to make a positive statement about their feelings on American involvement in Vietnam. However, they found in Mayday camp an attitude and strategy as repulsive as the one they had come to protest.

The Mayday leaders, the youngsters said, planned to get drums of oil, set them afire, and roll the flaming stuff into busy intersections at rush hour on Mayday. The boy and girl told of horrid plans to load up teenagers on drugs, then hurl them into assaults on police, hoping that panic would drive the officers into killing some of the youths. This would shift blame to the police, and lay foundations for charging the whole disaster was a "police riot." Further, said the youngsters, the Mayday leaders wanted some of the demonstrators positioned on slopes above George Washington Parkway, from where they would throw stones on passing cars below.

The interview with the refugees from Mayday camp shook me severely. Back in Birmingham, I had read stories about the protest movement in America. But there they had not thundered over me. Now, in Washington, I was beginning to believe that several thousand kids might actually be able to shut down the United States government! That thought was accompanied by another, telling me I was one of those responsible for preventing the overthrow.

Previously, I had thought myself buttressed by a healthy skepticism when it came to tall tales. Now, though, something was telling me I was in a vastly bigger league, and that the skirmishes fought here were for keeps. Thus the process began by which distrust, suspicion of those labeled *enemy* and *opponent* would fester. Fear was setting in, with a mixture of indignation and anger. Superaide was aborning!

And a few weeks later, I was appointed to the job at the White House.

There I learned another component necessary to the raising of Superaide: hard, cold pragmatism. The survival strategy (already noted) did its part in contributing to what struck me as utter pragmatism. And so did the apparent plan to follow a line of consensus politics. Whatever the case and motivation, the impression settling over me as a political greenhorn was that preference must be given always to the scheme or idea that produces concrete results. High ideals seemed costly luxury in the Washington gladiatorial arena—luxury whose indulgence might bring annihilation!

Our office had become something of a focal point for receiving communications from dismayed conservatives. We handled mail and telephone calls from people unhappy with the administration's version of welfare reform, which contained a provision resembling a guaranteed annual income. We conversed with constituents disturbed by Nixon's toying with the idea of federal aid for parochial schools. And China—I lost count of the number of letters and calls I took from ideological conservatives absolutely strung out over the President's courting of the People's Republic. After all, these were all matters on which the conservative voters had thought they had properly read Richard Nixon.

Throughout 1971, the White House was holding to a rigid, unbendable stance on the economy: Mr. Nixon was unalterably opposed to government intervention in the economy; there would be no wage and price controls. That was the position most expected Nixon to take, since he was identified with the conservative view.

On August 15, 1971, my family and I were eating

Sunday dinner. Summer had doused the rambling
field behind our house with a deep green. I looked
forward to an afternoon of romping through the
grass with my children. In the middle of the meal,
however, Harry Dent called and told me to get to the
White House. The President was going to make a
speech about the inflation-wracked economy. I, of
course, would make no substantial contribution to
the speech itself. However, someone had devised a
system wherein lower White House aides would telephone selected individuals around the country after a
Presidential speech, asking their opinion of what the
President said. If their remarks were favorable, our
job was to casually suggest they telegram the President with their support.

A large room had been designated somewhere
near the attic of the EOB as our headquarters. Tables full of telephones crowded the area. As I entered, I greeted the dozen or so other junior staffers
who sat at tables. A television monitor had been set
up in an adjoining room, and someone announced
the President was about to go on the air. The Presidential seal faded into Richard Nixon's face. It was
hard to believe he was just across a narrow street.
And it was also hard for me to believe what I was
hearing: After months of claiming the administration
viewed governmental intervention in the economy as
something in the category of Asian flu, Nixon was
announcing he was instituting wage and price controls!

The significance for me was not that I learned a
new lesson in economics. The political or economic
rightness of the move was not at issue in my mind
that evening. What was at issue was a new principle

of operation shaping up in Superaide's mind: If a cherished value gets in the way of positive action in Washington, it's the value that must go.

This may not have been at all the way Richard Nixon or his senior advisors approached the problem. But to a newly hatching Superaide, that seemed the logical inference.

I must concede a certain admiration for Nixon's boldness on some issues. He understood he could do things a liberal president would be lynched for doing, and Nixon faced up to that responsibility. For there is certainly a place for a measure of policy pragmatism in government. Flexibility is a requirement.

The tragedy of the first Nixon term, however, was that as the philosophy of pragmatism (perhaps even limited) passed through the White House Warp, it was as if a moderate glimmer of light were fed into a laser. The result was a devastating, cutting amplification in the form of generalization.

A further bending and intensification of the searing light came about as it was touched by the stinging flames of the political polarization of the period. Perhaps those who had been around awhile understood what was happening, and how to dodge the corrupting beam. But for many young or inexperienced or morally neutered Superaides, policy pragmatism was generalized and carried over into ethical pragmatism. It was often too easy to go from the line of reasoning that whatever policy would help the nation should be followed, to the idea that whatever was done to keep the administration in office was just as acceptable. The White House Warp had already convinced a hefty portion of Superaides that the administration's survival was nearly synonymous with that of the nation, anyway.

It seemed to me that many of the Superaides had come to their jobs with a mixture of anger and fear. The late sixties with its burning campuses and raging riots had staggered the entire country. Some of my colleagues had been in Washington as columns of sooty smoke had risen over the city and fires had burned short blocks from the White House. These people burned now with a determination to never let such happen again. *They* were in the place of responsibility now. *Time* magazine would later note "The Cooling of America." But fires, moral as well as physical, often burn out of control.

The problem with being young and inexperienced in the White House is that one is attempting to put into practice skills he is only then being schooled in. The newcomer to Washington assumes that what he observes as principle and practice from his tiny nook, is and has been normative. There is no school for White House Superaides save the White House itself. Then, of course, it's a bit late. Again, Reedy is right in contending that novitiates have no business in the place. My sudden schooling kept suggesting now and then that being pragmatic was at times more important than being honorable, since there might be a time when honor would dictate political suicide. The White House Warp made that appear as national suicide.

The problem may have been at the point of defining *honorable*. Without absolute standards of morality, definitions are up in the air. Policy pragmatism—*yes!* Moral pragmatism—*no!* Unless the distinction can be drawn, unless the current ethical relativism propelling RIGHT and LEFT is abandoned, we are destined to repeat Watergates. It will trap even those who decry it the most. They may be especially vulnerable, since they may be convinced of their own invulnerability.

The attitudes of the White House, circa 1969–1973, seethed in that era in which infantile abandon was mistaken for freedom—an era still with us. In humanity's passion to enthrone the counterfeit gods of its own making, it has lost sight of the absolute nature of the God of the universe. Mankind, in the words of Duncan Williams, in his brilliant book *Trousered Apes,* is struggling to be its own lawmaker, its own aesthete. But without the Lord of the universe we have no idea what honor and justice and righteousness look like!

Oddly, the administration was mouthing quite often about this God of the universe. But, as the next chapter will say, there is ample evidence this was part of the larger pragmatism. God could be worshiped in the East Room on Sunday, and lies be told in the press room on Monday. Pragmatism permitted no question about contradictions. It dictated that whatever had to be done to maintain power—be it the worship of God or the twisting of information—it should be done.

Bill Moyers, in a *Newsweek* article, September 23, 1974, was quite right in urging caution when it comes to politicians who convey the image they speak the mind of God. The pragmatic religion of the White House world was plagued by the notion that the most important element was the mouthing of religiosity. The talk was abundant, the study of the absolute ethical principles revealed in the Bible was virtually nonexistent. If one is going to talk about God, he ought at least to know something about the God he talks about. Should a President, a Superaide, be a theologian, then? The question is moot. They already are, by virtue of the fact they are human beings.

There is a certain irony in the fact we make great claims of the principles of the Constitution stemming from the high ethics of Christianity. Yet, we are quite satisfied to learn much about the child and neglect the mother! Perhaps a clearer understanding of the biblical philosophy of man and his behavior would provide a more comprehensive grasp of the meaning of the Constitution and the Bill of Rights. Rules and regulations can be twisted easiest when there is no understanding of why they are given, or what constitutes their foundations.

One of the questions I have wrestled with most fiercely is why I couldn't see all this while I was in the White House. Why was I so bent on taking the characteristics of Superaide?

Certainly one of the reasons was that I had an infection of what is known as the White House disease: DED (Dissent Equals Disloyalty). It is a strain of Potomac Fever. But the germ takes its own unique form after having been incubated in the White House. As outside attacks mounted on the President and his warriors, it seemed clear there were enough enemies to tell us where we were wrong. Our job was to lock arms and withstand the assaults. A questioning spirit was choked out by DED.

The junior aide is particularly vulnerable. That level White House staffer is the person who will prepare the memoranda, follow up on directives stemming from sessions in the Oval Office, without the benefit of having been there. Many times, I would watch Harry Dent return to our corner of the EOB from the Presidential presence. Dent would be fairly glowing as the office staff assembled in an attempt to catch some of the light. "The President wants us to . . ." Dent would say, and our pens would fly over our note pads, jotting every instruction.

The ready surrender stemmed from the fact that to be Superaide, one had to make abject obedience to the awesome authorities above him a constant practice. Lower-level Superaides worked on the assumption that the orders they received from superiors were honorable, legal—or at least tolerable. It's possible some of the junior aides trapped in the Watergate mud got in the dilemma because they made assumptions of legitimacy about their orders they really were not safe to make.

During the period of the publication of the Pentagon Papers, for example, I sensed from my lowly perch a kind of panic at the higher rungs. Rumors descended: The next thing to go will be our negotiating position on Vietnam, or the points we are willing to concede in the Strategic Arms Limitation Talks (SALT). In such a furious pitch of rumor and fear, one can imagine a senior aide saying to a deputy, "We suspect that Daniel Ellsberg is an agent. The security of this country rests on your finding out everything you can about him." (I selected the case of Dr. Ellsberg here only because of its notoriety. I have no idea if the factors discussed here played into that particular situation.)

Perhaps it sounds hokey—right out of Ian Fleming. But it sounds horribly real when one is young and awed and suffering from DED, the Warp, the passion to be Superaide *all at once*. So the junior aide assumes that his bosses have met, that CIA supersecret reports have been digested, the FBI consulted, and that a course of action has been decided upon which he must implement. The moral considerations of what must be done may have little or no bearing. The Warp is persistent in giving the idea that what happens at 1600 Pennsylvania Avenue transcends the fine points of ethics.

Professor Stanley Milgram's studies in human response to authority describe quite well what happens to Superaide in the White House. Frighteningly, Dr. Milgram found that people were willing to bring suffering on others if they were ordered to do so by significant authority. In his book *Obedience to Authority,* Professor Milgram says:

> . . . ordinary people, simply doing their jobs, and without any particular hostility on their part, can become agents in a terrible destructive process. Moreover, even when the destructive effects of their work become patently clear, and they are asked to carry out actions incompatible with fundamental standards of morality, relatively few people have the resources needed to resist authority . . . .

Oddly, Superaide's identity is tied to its absorption into the mass identity of the White House. Were it not for the embellishments of power and fame that it is his job to maintain (and enjoy), he would be just another person in a crowded city. I remember visiting the White House before joining its staff. I stood in line with hundreds of other tourists at the East Gate. Then I remember attending meetings in the East

Wing after joining the staff. I would pass the tourists, always conscious of an identity they did not possess. And I always felt very vulnerable with that identity. It was as transitory as the fanning of the humming-bird's wings. How terrifying: to have one's identity wrapped up in a mass that would disappear. For even if I didn't get fired, Nixon would not be the President forever.

In retrospect, there was something Hindu about it. One found oneself only after freedom from being re-born out in the world of pain, and being merged into the mass of the ultimate, the White House. The feel-ing also had impact on the way Superaide handled his response to authority. "The disappearance of a sense of responsibility is the most far-reaching conse-quence of submission to authority," Milgram says. From inside, the White House always looked big enough to absorb the consequences of any action!

But obedience to authority is essential for an or-dered society. The question one must face, whether in the White House or sweat house (at times they are synonymous!), is this: To which authority will I sur-render myself? Those who fret about separation of religion and ideas of deity from institutions of gov-ernment may as well save their agony. There are gods in the White House whether one likes it or not. For every time a person asks the question of author-ity in his life, he's seeking to define *his* god. And every time a course of decision is accepted and an-other rejected, one god takes over in the place of the other. I am not unaware of the dangers of cultural religion. But I am also conscious of the fact that if people are bound inevitably to follow after some god, it ought to be the real One!

To put it another way: Superaide can answer adequately the question of all secondary authority only after he has things straight with prime, or ultimate Authority.

In the White House, Superaide is likely to surrender so utterly because he sees himself as a necessary subject occupying a necessary niche in an institution necessary to society's survival. But if Superaide belongs to God, he should be subject to God's order, which transcends human hierarchies. Again, what is needed here is not another divine-right potentate announcing God has told him to do this or that, but a person whose life is steered by the strong currents of love and mercy and justice and peace flowing from God's Word. If government is the art of serving society by helping it pull together on such ideals, then those working in government ought to have commitments to the Giver of the ideals. This means cutting loose from allegiance to authorities whose *only* concern is the pragmatics of keeping alive sham structures it passes off as essential for society's survival, authorities which have not been tempered by allegiance to Him who beckons and empowers one to live justly.

Perhaps this sounds too idealistic. But two years in the White House makes one hunger for an articulation of ideals, fearing that a certain cultural weariness has blunted the quest for the best. Besides, commitment to God's order first is the best guarantee of the survival of ordered society. "Seek first the kingdom of God and His righteousness and these things will be added to you" said Jesus (*see* Matthew 6:-33).

Perhaps the most devastating consequence of the

climb to Superaide on the individual is the loss (or severe curtailment) of the individual's critical faculties. As a journalist specializing in covering the church, I prided myself too much on the ability to raise biting questions. In the White House, I felt so completely out of my orbit, I often kept my mouth shut. If the critical faculties are not used often, they get creaky, like a proficiency in a foreign language. Where once the first thing that popped into the mind was a question, there is after a while only blank assent. The phenomenon is not a conspired brainwashing; the net effect, however, can come perilously close to being that.

The blunting of my critical faculties was helped along by some of my assignments. Late in 1971 and well into 1972, I was assigned, through the White House speakers bureau, to campus appearances. By mid-1972, I was speaking on two or three major campuses a week. One day in Chicago, for example, I spoke at three institutions, then journeyed to Milwaukee for engagements at Marquette University.

Following each speech, there would be a discussion period, when I would be asked questions on everything from tax reform to our current attitudes toward Bhutan. I was not an economist, but I would find myself in the thicket of a debate with graduate students in economics. In fact, I was not an expert in any of the fields I talked about, yet I had to wear the mask of the universal specialist!

Once, in Salt Lake City, I was scheduled to appear on a radio talk show. Listeners would call in with their questions. The affair flowed smoothly until midpoint. Then, a young voice came on the line with the question, "Do you enjoy napalming babies?"

Cleverness, profundity all departed me. I was ambushed. Bloody, I stuttered and stammered until the caller, in mercy, released me. I left the studio angry. I would never be trapped again. My efforts would be dedicated to the great end of the pithy, all-encompassing answer. I would always be ready to assert, defend. *Ready*. That was it. I would always be *ready*.

My crutch was a fat looseleaf binder crammed with facts about the administration stance on hundreds of issues. The briefing book was three inches thick. It was my brain in remote. I spent the rest of 1972 like a student preparing for perpetual final exams. I memorized tiny tidbits of data, coupling them with zippy sentences. I prayed for long trips, so I would have extra time on the airplane to plow through my briefing book.

And so it happened. I was so busy getting ready to defend myself against the questions of others, I ceased being critical about the issues myself. They were nothing more than statistics to remember, dates to cough up at the right moment. They blurred from concerns of the nation's life to symbols of my success or failure as Superaide. To raise questions myself would be fatal, I thought, since I knew only the responses given in the briefing book.

So Superaide was aborning. He was closemouthed, skeptical of the press, and distrustful in general, pragmatic, submissive to his superiors in a way bordering on blindness, and increasingly uncritical of his environment or philosophies.

At home, he was grouchy, testy, tense, difficult to live with. And much later—after his liberation from playing Superaide—it would occur to him midst deep

pain that he had spent more in commitment to playing *that* role that he had been willing to give—up to
that point—in commitment to his Lord.

Nevertheless, Superaide felt the tender skin of the
egg cracking. And out he stepped.

4

Of Politicians and Preachers

Halfway through the 1972 campaign, somebody at the Committee to Re-elect the President (CRP) remembered the clergy. Word was out that Senator George McGovern's campaign had something called Evangelicals for McGovern, led, we understood, by evangelist Tom Skinner. The CRP strategists noted our side had no such tool, and they wondered how we could do our political gardening without it. Someone else at CRP knew I was an ordained minister, and asked me for recommendations on getting pro-Nixon preachers into the campaign.

CRP's request to me for political advice was not all that strange. I had already learned that some politicians in Washington felt kinship with clergymen. The politicians concluded that a man who could meld all the divergent views in the average church into a marching, cooperating unit, must possess skills of political artistry. Of course, it was overlooked that miracles of Christian unity are brought about by the Holy Spirit. Nevertheless, when I conceded that I had few qualifications in politics for being attached to Harry Dent's White House political liaison office, the only reply had been a chuckle and a question: "How long have you been a Baptist preacher. . . ?"

A phenomenon I call the Overkill Syndrome probably affected CRP's thinking about the clergy and the campaign. For example, there would be occasional briefings for the White House staff on general campaign strategy, conducted by high CRP officials. The Executive Office Building auditorium, where the briefings were sometimes held, would have its walls dressed with posters carrying a remark by McGovern political aide Gary Hart. In effect, Hart had said that the Nixon people would somewhere leave a flank exposed. The McGovern camp would find that flank, and Nixon would be zilched. Perhaps someone concluded that the Nixon effort was exposed on the religious flank. The Overkill Syndrome dictates all flanks be covered twice. Something, therefore, had to be done about the preachers, it appeared.

After consulting with some of my clergy-oriented friends in Washington, we submitted a position paper to Clark MacGregor, who had replaced John Mitchell as head of the Nixon campaign. In the paper, we noted the necessity of communicating with the American religious community. We felt, however, that we should not attempt to organize ministers into political campaign units. Instead, we suggested, the White House should conduct a series of issue briefings for religious leaders. CRP would pay expenses, and the people invited would be told of that arrangement in advance. No mention of the campaign should be made at the White House briefing, we thought, except to say to the clergymen that in light of the election we felt they would like to be able to question policy-makers on the administration stance on various issues.

The proposal was accepted, and several briefings

were held. Weeks later, I was in Dallas for a speech, and had stopped at the office of an old friend—Gil Stricklin, of the Baptist General Convention of Texas. Gil's secretary buzzed him that the White House was trying to reach me. Gordon Strachan, an aide to White House Chief-of-Staff Bob Haldeman, told me the powers-that-were had determined we needed a full-fledged clergy organization, and that CRP was putting aboard a man to get the project rolling. I expressed my disagreement and reservations, but the decision was clearly irrevocable.

CRP planned a media luncheon, in which the establishment of the clergy organization would be announced. I knew many of the religious leaders invited to the meet, so I slipped in for the luncheon, which was held at a Washington hotel. Dr. Harold Ockenga, the noted Boston clergyman, was chairman. After the meal, he began detailing to the audience the reasons for assembling the ministers. As it became apparent that the purpose of the luncheon was to announce formation of a clergy-for-Nixon organization, Dr. John Bisagno, paster of Houston's First Baptist Church, rose to his feet. No one, he said, had informed him he was coming to Washington to join a political organization. He thought he was coming simply for a briefing. Quickly, other clergymen joined Bisagno in disassociating themselves from a campaign organization. Overkill had struck again. Dr. Ockenga was rattled. It was apparent he thought invitational telegrams had spelled out the reason for the meeting. Some of the ministers present were outright incensed, feeling they had been manipulated. Their feelings came across quite clearly on the evening news.

If the preachers were manipulated, it wasn't the first time such happened in Washington. And the practice is not limited to the White House. Many a politician has learned that he can defuse the thorniest of issues with the right religious codewords, or by making God appear the prime advocate of the position the politician supports.

Was, then, the practice of holding worship services at the White House part of this manipulation of religion for political ends? The answer to that one is a very firm *yes* or *no,* depending on whom the question is asked about.

Richard Nixon seemed to hold, subconsciously at least, that cultural values were more important than personal ones. Cultural values, in this scheme, were apparently measured by their surface appearance— their PR, if you will. This, perhaps, is the reason a man who could preside over the worship service in the East Room on Sunday, could say the shocking things on the Watergate tapes in the Oval Office on Monday. In reality, of course, the personal value has to precede the cultural. A culture is nothing more than the sum of individual minds which make it up. But through the White House Warp, it seemed the most important thing was the projection of the right ethical image. If the proper cultural values were projected, the idea seemed to be that the nation would absorb them through osmosis of some sort.

Nixon obviously believed religion to be a vital component for a healthy civilization. Whether this stemmed from pragmatism like that of Toynbee, who sees religion as cultural glue, or personal conviction, I do not know. Nevertheless, Richard Nixon, the Quaker from Whittier, was going to contribute to history and culture by leading in the revival of moral values through a public stress on religion. This compounds the tragedy of Nixon, since the history books will have to deal with Watergate, the transcripts, along with the virtuous.

If it is difficult to arrive at a sharp understanding of Nixon's philosophy of White House worship services, the attitude of many of us Superaides was not hard to decipher. Too often, we lapsed into viewing the East Room service as a good "stroking opportunity." *Stroking* (in the convoluted White House terminology) was any act by which one appeased and rewarded friends, or cooled offended nerves. The penultimate stroking opportunity was an invitation to a state dinner, with the President and a foreign head of state. As I understood it, the worship service was a distance down the list. Folks who weren't worthy of a state dinner were sometimes invited to a worship service. There were, of course, some lucky ones who got it all.

Since the White House Warp had blurred some of my attitudes, I raised no objection when asked to call state political chairmen for lists of people they would like to have invited to the worship services. Superaide was proficient with the telephone, less proficient with the questions.

Was every religious concern in the White House of the manipulative variety? Absolutely not. I have already alluded to the existence of the White House staff-prayer breakfast. We were very interested that our group not become a matter of public knowledge. Opportunities arose for articles to be written about our being together, but they were declined. In fact, it's possible our attendances would have been higher had we pushed harder within the Executive Branch itself to let people know we were meeting. The only so-called advertisement was a brief memorandum I circulated each week to those who attended or expressed an interest.

There were times when our small prayer fellowship expanded considerably. For example, when the acting chief of state from Cambodia visited Washington, we invited him and his entourage to our prayer breakfast. A number of cabinet members also attended. On another occasion, Sammy Davis, Jr., was visiting one of the prayer group regulars on other business, and we invited him to sit in with us. On yet another day, Billy Graham was our guest, and again the room overflowed.

Talk of religion, sincerity, and the White House invariably raises the subject of Charles Colson. Since leaving the White House, I have been asked dozens of times if I knew Colson, and, if his post-Watergate religious experience was real, in my opinion. The answer to both questions is *yes*.

I did not know Colson well in our White House days. He was on the senior staff, I was at the bottom professional rung, and we had no contact. But I had feelings about Colson. I didn't like him. Rather, I didn't like the way he looked. Once, during the Republican National Convention in Miami Beach, I watched him amble across the pool deck at our hotel. A smugness seemed to shout out from his face. I believed most of the nasty things I had read about the man.

So when I heard about the Colson conversion, I reacted with cautious happiness. I never knew the day would come when I would see for myself, first-hand.

The first contact I had with Colson after leaving Washington was in Febrauary 1973. I had gone back to the city for the National Prayer Breakfast. I walked into the Washington Hilton Hotel, and a friend from the Fellowship Foundation asked if I would like to see Colson. Of course, I replied.

I had written Chuck Colson a letter after hearing of his discovery of Christ, telling him I would be praying for him. As I walked into the room that night, I knew Colson would not recognize me, but I hoped he would remember the letter.

A dozen or so men were sitting in a circle with Chuck, who was doing the talking. I introduced myself, and Chuck gave me a slight smile and kept speaking. Within five minutes, he was finished, and asked me to lead in prayer. I pronounced an *Amen,* and turned to leave the room, thinking I would catch Colson after everyone else had spoken to him. But he bounded over to where I was, and embraced me.

The first thought that shot through my mind was, "This isn't the Chuck Colson I have known." There was no longer a smugness in his demeanor. There was warm openness. Somewhere the tough marine who had told his staff he would walk over his grand-mother for the reelection of Richard Nixon had been transformed into a different personality. I felt I might actually be able to trust my own grandmother with Colson. From that day forward, whenever the Colson question came up as I spoke to groups, I would tell them I felt he was real.

I had no more contact with Colson after meeting him in Washington. I watched as he entered a guilty plea in matters relating to the Ellsberg break-in, and began serving a jail sentence. In fact, I had tried to be true to my commitment to pray for Chuck, and kept up with the events of his life. But I felt sure that would be the extent of my involvement.

In the fall of 1974, I got a call from Doug Coe, a Washington layman, who, with Senator Harold Hughes, had played the significant role of discipling Colson in his new commitment to Christ.

"They're moving Chuck to the Federal Prison Camp at Maxwell Air Force Base," said Doug. Maxwell was only 150 miles north of my home. Doug asked me if I would begin visiting Chuck regularly. The request thrilled me. If Chuck Colson's acceptance of Christ had only been a maneuver aimed at eliciting mercy, the grueling tests of prison would bring the sham to the surface.

The first fifteen minutes with Colson convinced me the man was for real. I had remembered Chuck as having been always well tailored in executive pinstripes. Now he greeted me in rumpled prison clothes. A man who once had the ear of the President of the United States now worked in the prison laundry.

But there was a calm serenity about the man. And one day he told me, "I'm happier here than I ever was in the White House, because here I have the Lord."

On later visits, I would learn more and more of Chuck's ministry in the prison. He had developed a probing compassion for his colleagues, and a deep concern for the dehumanizing rigors of prison life. We talked often of Jesus' preoccupation with captives. Chuck sought to deal with everyone who came

to him, whether they were check forgers or embez-
zlers. "Prison is supposed to be a place where you
have nothing but time on your hands, but I don't
have enough time," he chuckled one day.

But I had also been asked questions about the personal commitment of Richard Nixon. On a couple of
occasions I thought I had opportunity to observe this
very private aspect of a very private man. A few
weeks before the China trip in 1972, Rep. John
Buchanan of Tennessee and I decided to try to rally
as much of the nation as possible to pray for Nixon's
trip. I had already handled a good bit of the mail
spewing into the White House from conservatives
who were upset by the opening to China, and understood the division in people's minds. But Buchanan
and I had a dream: Surely, the nation could unite in
asking that whatever possibilities of good existed in
the trip would be realized; and, we thought, most
people would be at least willing to pray for Nixon's
safety. I told Harry Dent what Buchanan and I were
doing, and he mentioned it to an aide of Bob Haldeman. We assumed that was as close to the Oval Office as the project would get.

Since the journey was only six weeks off, we were
faced with the massive chore of communicating the
idea to the country. I talked with several prominent
Americans like Pat Boone and football coach Tom
Landry. They agreed to mention the project in public
appearances. Through the Fellowship Foundation,
which sponsors the National Prayer Breakfast, forty
governors and one hundred mayors agreed to issue
public proclamations calling for days of prayer in
their states and localities.

As far as I know, the higher-ups in the White

House who had been aware of Prayers for Peking had probably forgotten about it. Then one morning I arrived at the White House to find Harry Dent with an order which had come from Peking. We were told to prepare a summary of everything that had been done to get the nation praying for the trip, and dispatch the report via courier to Alaska, where the President would stop on his way back to Washington. The impression we drew was that Nixon wanted to digest the material on the way back.

I have often wondered what motivated that request. Was it a human being reaching out from the spinning vortex of history-making, groping for assurance of God's blessing and presence? Or, was it a canny politician trying to gauge political support by the number of people willing to pray for him?

But then there was that day with Oral Roberts. The evangelist had been invited in for a get-acquainted meeting with Nixon. Often, I helped coordinate visits by religious leaders, and had worked on a briefing paper for the President. Harry Dent had been designated staff man to sit in on the meeting but was sent out of town. I was tabbed to attend the session, and to host Roberts through the day. Nixon and Roberts had a pleasant half-hour conversation.

Then, at the conclusion, Roberts said, "Mr. President, I want to pray for you, then I want you to pray for me." Further, suggested Roberts, we should hold hands to strengthen our fellowship. We moved out onto the big blue rug in front of Nixon's desk, standing on the Presidential seal woven into the fabric.

Nixon and Roberts grasped hands, and Roberts held one of mine. But Nixon did not complete the circle by taking my other hand. It was just as well. The hand had a marked shake by now. All I could think was, "I didn't write the President a prayer!" I remember Steve Bull, the Presidential doorkeeper, cracking the door to signal the end of the meeting. It's a wonder the poor guy didn't panic, thinking he was watching a scene from the novel *The Night of Camp David* in which a President loses his balance. But Steve discreetly slipped back into the reception room.

Now it was Nixon's turn to pray. It was a simple, non-amateurish prayer. He had clearly done it before. One suspects he has done it often since. I relish thinking that midst all the garbage on the Nixon tapes, there will be at least one prayer.

Still, Nixon had some reluctance to talk in public about his personal relationship with God. No President, however, seems able to hit a happy medium here. Gerald Ford, in the early days of his Presidency, was criticized for saying *God* too much. But there were times when I genuinely felt Nixon was struggling to share something of his inner relationships, but couldn't leap the imposing barrier of his inverted personality.

I sensed this during Nixon's farewell to his staff. The deepest I ever felt it was when he addressed the National Prayer Breakfast in February 1974. Nixon had been in the dark Watergate jungle for more than a year, while America was wandering down the ragged streets of Disclosureville. And much of that disclosure was about a side of Nixon he had tried desperately to pretend in public didn't exist. Several of us that morning thought Nixon would surely open up, and talk about a newfound sense of reliance on

God. But he didn't. Later that day at lunch with several others who had attended the breakfast that morning, I found we all picked up signals Nixon was struggling very hard to say something he did not know how to say.

Many wondered if Nixon ever opened up with Billy Graham. The evangelist, of course, has been accused of getting too close to the politicians, or of letting himself be used. There is that possibility, of course, and I suspect Billy Graham knows that better than anyone.

But I left the White House with respect and even admiration for Graham. He's not stupid. He understands his vulnerability in reaching out to those at the highest levels of government. But Graham probably understands, too, that he may be the only preacher in America who can get to such people and their families.

There is a certain fashionableness in ministering to the poor, the prostitute, and the prisoner—and I pray that will not be a passing fad. But one's image is threatened if he tries to reach out to a publican, especially publicans whose Gallup ratings are not too high. Had Gallup been polling in the days of the incarnate Jesus, Matthew the publican would have been at the bottom of the chart. Yet Jesus selected him as a disciple, just as He had extended mercy to blind beggars. I really don't see how Billy Graham can be true to Jesus and do anything but minister to those with whom he comes in contact. Pastoring a politician may mean you yourself get labeled a crook. Which is precisely what they called Jesus as He hung between two thieves. I admire Billy Graham for taking the risk of a lousy label!

Besides, if Graham has been taken, he's not the only one. Evangelicals, perhaps, were among those most shocked by Nixon's language on the tapes. But the shock probably wouldn't have been so great had we evangelicals not been so eager to adopt Nixon as one of our own. Throughout history, we have been far too willing to read into leaders convictions they don't hold. Some of the founding fathers, for example, were deists, with vague abstract notions about God. Leading the pack was Thomas Jefferson, framer of the Constitution, which is sometimes called a "Christian" document. Nevertheless, these vague religionists come out in some evangelical (and otherwise) minds as spiritual ancestors of Charles Spurgeon and Dwight L. Moody!

Nor are many modern politicians all that interested in turning away such misconceptions about their religious convictions. The Southern Baptist vote alone could make the difference in a narrow national election!

Mistakes are going to be made in the thorny relationship between religion and politics. But that doesn't give Christians license to isolate themselves from the political process. Nor does it give politicians a blanket okay to turn off God.

The Gospel, after all, is for sinners.

5

The Geist in the White House

The regular White House tours stay out of the West
Wing, the business end of the place. Often, then,
when friends came to town, I would walk them over
to the west basement and through the corridors so
electrified with important-looking activity. If the
President was working outside the Oval Office, a vel-
vet rope was hung across the big doorway to the
room, and the door left open. The room would be on
display for the selected viewers. I never tired of the
reactions of my guests, for it seemed to me often they
felt something bordering on mystical experience.

For example, conversation to that point would
click off at banter pace. But as the visitors glimpsed
the office, the talk would tatter off into forgotten little whispers. Frequently, there would be tears. Facial
expressions would shift to awe, as if we had stepped
from a Roman back alley into the Sistine Chapel.
And always, there would be reverential silence.

George Reedy says in *The Twilight of the Presidency* that he believes ". . . the only real blas-
phemy—the deadliest of sins—is the deification of
mortals and the sanctification of human institutions.
We are guilty of that sin and retribution is certain."
Reedy, of course, was talking about the Presidency. I

can't help but wonder: Was Watergate the "retribution"?

Retribution for what? One might ask this quite
reasonably. The answer: human messianism, idolatry. In the nonreligion of the secular city, humanity
has had little recourse but to place its faith in the
disposable deities it makes with its own hands. For
Americans, at least, is it possible the Presidency has
become the pinnacle of a neo-Gnostic system in
which the demiurges serving the throne are human
institutions and technologies, ranging from Cabinet
agencies to deodorants? Are these to change lives?

Speaking of disposable deities: The spectacle of
Nixon's banishment is reminiscent of the animistic
practice of throwing out the totem when the harvest
is slim. The national totem is exiled, and (we are
told) the "nightmare" of Watergate is over. *Poof!*
Like that.

Ready continues that the Presidency "must be
made human again." And I remember one day being
in Steve Bull's office on routine business. Bull, as
noted earlier, was Nixon's doorkeeper and chief run-
ner. His office was an anteroom to the Oval Office,
and a side door led directly from Bull's chamber into
the President's office. Now that door was slightly
ajar. I could see Nixon standing behind the big desk,
shuffling some papers and scratching furiously at his
nose. And I thought, *Presidents aren't allowed to do
that!* Television commentators made much of Nixon's sweating upper lip, his heavy beard. They also
had a great deal to say about Nixon's lack of "humanity," yet every time it crept out, it was ridiculed.
Why can't we accept Presidents as men with sweaty
upper lips and itching noses who sometimes misplace

their notes? I know: We have crowned them gods, and when they resist the annoyances of being human we are as shocked as would have been an ancient Egyptian holy man had he seen the jackal-god sneeze!

This aspect of the Presidency lending itself so readily to deification I call the *Geist*—the spirit. It is dangerously Wagnerian. Richard Wagner, the nineteenth-century German cultural freak, believed devoutly in the power of the German *Geist* as the world's redemptive force. Wagner saw his own artistic expression as the incarnate channel of such "salvation." His deism was a concoction of the worst of secular humanism and Greek mythology. "In Wagner's art," says Hans Kohn, in *The Mind of Germany,* "shapeless chaos triumphed over the gods." Thus, in Wagner's antitheology, the gods were weak and men strong.

But Wagner went the ultimate step. He concluded that not only was his art the saving force, but that he himself was the *Geist*—the very embodiment of this "redemptive" German spirit. On September 11, 1865, Wagner wrote in his diary: "I am the most German person (*der deutscheste Mensch*), I am the German spirit."

Certainly no American President has proclaimed himself American incarnate. But the Presidential mysticism has developed partly, anyway, from the passion of the nation to find its face—its representative figure. Collectively, Americans have developed a vicarious identification of their own character and capabilities with those of the President. The Dow Jones is not the only tool for calibrating the fortunes of the President in office. National morale rises and falls

with fluctuations in the Presidential *Geist*. So Mary
McGrory, the columnist, must have been full of the
Presidential religion when she reportedly told Patrick
Moynihan, upon the assassination of John F. Ken-
nedy, "We'll never laugh again." Was she suggesting
the spirit of laughter died with Kennedy?

Each President in recent years, of course, has had
his unique role to play in this scheme of human messianism. Probably none has sought it or been aware
of its full implications. The expectations placed on
the office and the personality traits demanded of a
person who makes the bloody marathon to the Presidency have as much to do with creating the Presidential *Geist* as anything. Once in the Oval Office, of
course, the immense power pulsating round the place
like a bright red aura breaks down a good bit of the
critical objectivity that may have been brought there.

Through several months of 1966–67, Arthur
Schlesinger, Jr., and Alfred de Grazia worked each
other over in debates on the Presidency. Some of the
discussion is recalled in Henry Fairlie's book, *The
Kennedy Promise*. In one of the conversations, de
Grazia said this:

> We have an officer called the President, who, con-
> sidering that our age is not religious, nevertheless
> begins to satisfy the divine aspects of the Roman
> Imperator . . . The President is believed to repre-
> sent the people, not in any ordinary sense, but in
> the most remarkable of ways, involving psychic
> waves, psychological projections, even the statistical
> proofs of scientoid professors who feel themselves
> immune from vulgar obsessions . . . .

The only point of disagreement with de Grazia is
his suggestion our age is not religious. Every age is

religious, for man is always in search of some kind of deity, and always winds up giving spiritual allegiance to something. It's just that ours is an age of "secular religion," when men look to themselves and their institutions for messiahs and temples. This is the purest form of antichrist, since antichrist is not only *against,* but is a *usurper* of, the role of the real Christ. And John says that the antichrist is here now, in spirit (1 John 4:3). No, I'm *not* saying the President of the United States is antichrist. The point is that there is a *spirit,* an *attitude,* which compels humanity to deify the profane, or material. And this process has a great deal to do with the cultivation of the Presidential *Geist.*

The tendency is not isolated in the web-infested cavern of twentieth-century thought. Fairlie recalls Walt Whitman's lines on the assassination of Lincoln:

> For you they call, the swaying mass, their eager
>   faces turning;
> Here Captain! dear father!

In 1841, Thomas Carlyle wrote that "the history of the world is but the biography of great men." Carlyle meant no doubt that the actions of great men set off historical currents and tides. But the history of human spirit far below the level of event, is shaped by the intangible qualities of the great men and the positions they occupy. Call it *charisma, Geist,* or whatever, but it exists in a spiritual context.

Take, for example, the correlation between the rise of John Kennedy and the mysticism of youth. "Nearly everything about Kennedy and his brief stay at the White House," said pollster Lou Harris, "symbolized the American worship of things young . . . The young were beautiful and to be beautiful you had to stay young" (in *The Anguish of Change*). But the Kennedy *Geist* didn't merely represent the worship of things young; it cultivated, sparked it. Another observation by Harris shows how deeply mystical an effect the Presidential *Geist* can have on society:

When Lee Harvey Oswald shattered Kennedy's skull from his perch in the Dallas Bookmart in 1963, he shattered perhaps the most powerful symbol of youth produced by the twentieth century . . . . The identification of people everywhere with the hope and vibrance that flows from being young had been wiped out.

It is no wonder, then, America has tried so hard to cling to the Kennedy memory. For many, he was not simply a President, but a *spiritual* force. In an article in the August 17, 1962, issue of *The Nation,* Mary Paul lamented "the amassing by [President Kennedy] of personal power; and—most insidious of all—the irrational world-wide identification of him with the country as a whole . . . Mr. Kennedy has become synonymous with the United States; his victories are American victories; his health, American health; his family, his hobbies, his likes and dislikes, become symbolic of the country." Is there something here reminiscent of Wagner's statement that he was the "most German" of the Germans? Kennedy never claimed to be the representative American. He didn't have to; the *Geist* saw to that.

The Eisenhower Presidency had its distinctive *Geist*. "Ike" was the way President Eisenhower was endearingly addressed by the nation. But no one would have used the term in the Oval Office. It was more a title to be bestowed in the abstract manner someone addresses a powerful benevolent deity. Some people, for example, call God "The Man Upstairs" in the same way. Indeed, if there were a real Uncle Sam, no one would call him that to his face.

Eisenhower was a father figure in an age when post-war America was tipping into cultural adolescence. Once in an interview, President Nixon seemed to be saying that the American people were like children needing to be led. Press reaction was acrid and massive. Nixon, perhaps, was merely reflecting what he had learned about President and people while serving as Eisenhower's vice-president. And Eisenhower could have gotten away with the statement, because of the time in which it was made, if nothing else. The Eisenhower *Geist* was fatherly, patriarchal in a period when America was just growing up to the horrors of a nuclear era. Ike was clearly identified as a white hat. He was the good god of the West to the devil manifestations of the East: Stalin, Bulganin, Khrushchev.

It was during Lyndon Johnson's Presidency that the *Geist* got in trouble. In his caretaker term, when he was viewed as High Priest of the Kennedy *Geist,* it was in good order. During Johnson's elective term, however, the erosion took place. And it was not all the fault of Johnson. The *Geist* is always seen best against the backdrop of heavies on the other side. As noted above, Eisenhower had Khrushchev, Kennedy had Khrushchev and Castro. Before them, Roosevelt and Truman had Stalin and Hitler. But who did Johnson have? The dour, unspectacular Kosygin, hovered over by the dark eyebrows of Brezhnev, were now the lightweight "heavies" in the Soviet Union. Mao was still behind the Bamboo Curtain. The missile crisis had taken the hot air out of Castro—in the American mind, anyway. Ho Chi Minh might have been the heavy that could have set off the Johnson *Geist,* except something else was happening in America: the birth of the antihero.

The good guys and bad guys became confused in the nation's perception. The heroes were now the weak, vulnerable Dustin Hoffmans, bumbling through love trysts, in sharp contrast with the Errol Flynns, who, in a past age, had zapped the Huns, won the ladies without a single strand of hair losing its place. Bonnie and Clyde zoomed to heroic stature. The only invincible in the Johnson era was James Bond; only he was mere campish satire, not to be taken seriously. Ho Chi Minh, the flimsy little fighter from Indochina who stood up to the French and who was now standing up to the Americans, fell quite naturally into the hero category of the age of the antihero. Those who exalted him neatly overlooked the Stalinesque society he had raised in North Vietnam, and the inhumane tricks he used for land reform. In another age, Ho would have fallen into the villain lists, and America and her leader would have again been the good guys. Daily, the nation was teased with the idea that maybe, this time, their leader was the heavy. The impact on the *Geist* was devastating— especially since containment of communism in Asia via the Vietnam route was the linchpin of Johnson's foreign policy.

But the keystone in his domestic policy was the war on poverty. Here, for a while, there seemed real success. What credibility was lost for the *Geist* in the rotten jungles in Indochina might be retained through heroic efforts to liberate the poor at home. But soon the public saw the war on poverty going up in smoke in Washington, Newark, and Watts. As a mass, it could not understand the drive of rising expectations induced by the poverty war. Foreign policy seemed a dismal failure, domestic policy seemed a horrendous flop. Constantly—in media, on the streets, in institutions high and low—the *Geist* was being repudiated. No wonder Eric Goldman, who had served as an aide to Johnson, would write later in *The Tragedy of Lyndon Johnson:* "The story of Lyndon Johnson's Presidency is a story of tragedy in the ancient haunting sense of the word, the strong man overwhelmed by forces, from within and without." Thomas Altizer had told the country God was dead; now the *Geist* seemed dead too.

In such a time, Richard Nixon became President of the United States. Was the passion to restore the *Geist* the unconscious motive behind the effort to expand the power of the Executive? Was the revival of the *Geist* at the heart of Nixon's penchant to note every minute "first" of his Presidency? Early in President Nixon's first term, the White House police force was dressed briefly in "ceremonial uniforms like the household guard in a European court," in the words of columnists Evans and Novak, in their book, *Nixon in the White House.* Everywhere, there seemed a determination to restore to the Presidency something that had been lost.

And the Watergate coverup: How much did the desire to resuscitate the *Geist* have to do with that? Would Nixon have taken a different course had he not felt a compelling mission of his Presidency was to place the Executive back on its throne of glory? I can only raise questions, because I do not know what was in the deepest level of Nixon's thought processes in those days. But no one could work in the White House during that period without realizing that a major goal was the maximum glorification of the Presidency.

For example, I learned soon after starting work at the White House that the accepted form of referring to the Boss in memoranda was not *RN,* as I had used at first. It was always *The President.* Later on, in the 1972 campaign, a few commentators would note bumperstickers designed by the Committee to Re-elect the President would read RE-ELECT THE PRESIDENT, and not, RE-ELECT NIXON. Some of the commentators would suggest that CRP had decided Nixon was an essentially unloved character, and that the nation would vote for the President before they would Richard Nixon. Maybe the signs *really* read: RE-ELECT THE GEIST.

Let it be said emphatically that the United States needs a strong Presidency, just as it needs strong Legislative and Judicial branches. But there is a fine line between the acquisition of strength and the intoxication of the *Geist* affecting the President and virtually everyone in the White House.

Human messianism, of course, is a most unpartisan sin. If Nixon and the Republicans sought to build a messianism of the Presidency, many Democrats, in the company of Rousseau, have attempted a messianism of institutions. This was the root sin of the Great Society, when it was believed and preached that proper laws and institutions would bring miraculous alterations in American thought and behavior. But people are changed by the authentic Messiah, not by man-made counterfeits. The crushing despair of the late sixties and the ensuing national chaos came as much as anything when people saw that the claims made for governmental institutions were overdone. For what had been claimed was almost messianic in scope.

That was unfair to the institutions. For example, there might not have been so much disappointment with the Office of Economic Opportunity had the public been told from the outset, "This is a tool to *try* to treat the problem of poverty." Rather, the nation was led to believe that OEO was the cure-all, the messianic arm of redemption from the hell of being poor.

This is not to say we must cease making laws or raising institutions. It is to say we must stop being idolatrous about them. For idolatry is precisely where our secular humanism has led us, and the price we are paying as a society is bleeding us to death! Tragically, we have looked to men for our ultimates, rather than to God; we have bowed the knee to the laws of pragmatics and expediencies rather than to the absolute order of the Absolute Monarch of the universe. We have wanted Him around when He could lend us a political boost. But we have not permitted Him to be Lord of our political system. And, after all, "Lord" is His primary name (*see* Philippians 2:5–11).

It is a grave error to compare the historical role and position of the United States with that of ancient, theocratic Israel. America is *not* a covenant nation as was the Israel of the Prophet Amos. Nevertheless, his words penetrate to our own situation.

The prophet persists in pointing beyond earthly potentates, to the transcending God of the universe. He condemns the Israelites for measuring their security by the "hill of Samaria"—the representation of military might. Amos would rail against our modern absolute trust in arsenals and technology. He speared the hearts of the people because of their simplistic notion that since there was material prosperity, there was the automatic approval of God. Imagine the comments of Amos were he alive today and listening to a Presidential address pronouncing the arrival of the Promised Era because the GNP rose a point last quarter!

And Amos deplored the *Geist* giving undue glory to human leadership. This was at the heart of that exchange with Amaziah, the court priest, recorded in Amos 7. Amos refuses to tailor his preaching at Bethel for the tastes of King Jereboam. Amos has prophesied that Jereboam is going to be killed, and Israel taken captive. Such a message can't be allowed to get out, even at Bethel (God's house). It will make the leader appear weak; the nation will be depressed, since the leader is *Geist*. Amaziah, then, cries out to Amos: "Be off, you seer! Off with you to Judah! You can earn your living and do your prophesying there. But never prophesy again at Bethel, for this is the king's sanctuary, a royal palace" (Amos 7:11–14 NEB).

The Greeks had a word for the sin of Jereboam, and the modern sin which leads to the Presidential *Geist's* assuming religious proportions. That word is *hubris*. Paul Tillich thought the main subject of

Greek tragedy was the failure of man to concede he does not grasp the infinity of God. *Hubris* has not been a conscious sin of our political system. But that is its greatest danger. What we are not conscious of, we do not resist.

We need the *Geist* out of the White House, and a man in there. We must repent of the sin of *hubris,* in the full sense of repentance, which is a "turning away." Otherwise we will be carried away into the captivity of Watergates again and again!

6

The Breaking Point

Requiem Mass for Superaide began like a Bourbon Street funeral: blaring trumpets, glory, proud prancing.

It was November 8, 1972, the day after Nixon's landslide election. To me it had seemed the passion of the White House during all my stay there had been to sniff the savory spice of victory. That had been done and then some.

The night before, Irene and I had tried to attend the victory party at the Shoreham Hotel. But the crowd had been so heavy, we straggled back over to the White House to watch the celebration on television. Now, on the morning of the eighth, I was dutifully drowsy, proving my so-called loyalty. (No upward-bounding Superaide would dare sleep while the Big Man was passing through the rigors of re-election—no matter how paltry the odds. Besides, we were interested in going to bed only with the sure knowledge that we would be employed in January!)

Psychically, maybe, we felt we had to hold Nixon's hand. Anyone who has ever watched election returns on television knows that all that electronic gimmickry makes possible the fastest and most complete election reports. Yet, in that long night, someone in the

White House felt apparently it was our solemn duty to protect the sanctity of the returns by establishing our own election tabulation center. Some of us were assigned to sit at telephones for part of the evening, chatting with party people all over the country, getting results, and phoning them to the Oracle who would communicate the data to the President. In flashy irreverent moments, I thought it would be easier to watch television.

Now, the day after the long night's journey into the winner's circle, a meeting of the staff was called. Masses of red-eyed Superaides gathered with a mixed glee reminiscent of children who've been too long on a merry-go-round: The tendency was toward nausea, but it had been such fun!

Now Nixon himself strode onto the platform. For some it was a rare glimpse of the man for whom they had put everything on the line. At that point, some were not aware just how much they had strung out for Nixon's re-election. They would find out in the horrendous months ahead. But now there was no hint of that. The Warp was as fierce as tornadic winds.

Nixon congratulated the staff for its fine work. No President, he suggested, had had a better set of troops. We were able—strong and nice—the best— *superior*.

Then Bob Haldeman took the floor and asked for all our resignations.

They say that when Mussolini was led to the wall to face the firing squad, all he could utter was, "But . . . but . . . Mr. Colonel . . . !" And all I wanted to say was, "But . . . but . . . Mr. Haldeman . . . !"

The euphoria was blunted momentarily. The shock ebbed, however, as Superaides concluded the request was a mere formality. No one wanted to take seriously the bid to turn in his White House pass. Far in the background, of course, was a kind of *kamikaze* feeling: If the Big Boss can be better served by our suicides politically and professionally, then so be it.

We were even given packets showing us how to resign. A memorandum, written by some anonymous axman, informed us that it was expected personnel actions 'would be completed by December 15. The waiting phase would be "a time of some uncertainty," conceded the memo.

Some of us passed through the Christmas season without any direction or hints on future employment. It was a time for faith, which tended to slide midst the great heaves of silence from the personnel office. A friend joked wryly that he didn't know whether to run up Christmas bills or not. Another fretted that the silence from the personnel office might be a subtle way of telling him to find a job somewhere else. Once we had been the warriors girding the battlements with our might. Now we were galley slaves on the bottom deck and somebody was going to scuttle our ships!

I decided to take some of the complaints to the personnel office. An acquaintance there agreed the process was a painful one—something on the order of Chinese torture. But, he said, he knew of no possibilities in his own area. And, further, none of the half dozen or so men working on staffing were permitted to discuss their work with one another. So he knew of no assignments being pondered in other quarters of the personnel office.

Shakespeare's words in *King Henry IV* were now so immediate and so relevant, it stung.

> Ill-weaved ambition, how much thou art shrunk!
> When that this body did contain a spirit,
> A kingdom for it was too small a bound;
> But now two paces of the vilest earth
> Is room enough. . . .
>
> > Part I, Act V, scene 4

Those words had been spoken to a corpse—which was what I felt like.

So as the scramble for jobs escalated, I joined the fray. It was occurring to me I was not quite as cherished a member of the team as Henry Kissinger. Thus, I was seeing that if I wanted to hang on I would have to work at it. The chore centered largely on letting people outside the Harry Dent planet in the White House cosmos know that I existed. That was the plight of most low-level Superaides.

Then one lousy, dank day, I got a microscopic fleck of poison on my brain. It was a question: *Why, really, are you struggling so hard to stay here?* For the first time in nearly two years, cold, acrid objectivity was seeping into my psyche like leaking gas into a closed chamber. And as I sorted through the possible answers, they all seemed slim. Happiness was the end-all, I concluded, chipped out via prestige, the realization of ambition, a measure of affluence, a share of awesome power. Yes, that kind of happiness was the reason for my tenacious grip on the White House.

I nearly fainted when I reached the next plateau of my climb up objectivity mountain. For the new perspective showed me I had had all those components of "happiness" for two years, and I was as empty and desolate as ever! I came to understand that despite the achievement of a White House job, I was still groping. That was supposed to have done it, but I scanned the past months and realized I had been hoping to use the present position as simply a stepping-stone to the next one. There had been no settled contentment, no peace of spirit, just the same old restlessness. Worse—my life still seemed without a binding purpose.

The danger of questions is that one often leads to another. My suppression of critical faculties had caused me to turn off the allegations and rumors rising around the Watergate, the ITT scandal, and other matters.

But the opening of my mind—however slight—was enough to dampen my ability to turn off the rumors. The immediacy of it all came late one night when Carl Bernstein of the Washington *Post* called to see if I could supply information about Watergate. I could not conceive that anyone in the White House would get involved in such a travesty, and couldn't understand why the President didn't seize the initiative of investigating and exposing the background of the deed. I said so often within my tiny circle of friends on the staff. Now Bernstein was telling me he had picked up word I was one of the people on the staff really upset about Watergate. "Wonderful," I thought, "they've heard some of the things I've been saying in the staff mess, and understand me to be one of the white hats—one of the good guys." I floated on that happy conclusion until months later, when I read *All The President's Men,* the book by Bernstein and his partner Bob Woodward. In it, they describe the techniques they used to dig out the Watergate story. I was dashed when I read this paragraph:

> . . . the approach that seemed to work best was less than straightforward: A friend at the committee told us that you were disturbed by some of the things you saw going on there; that you would be a good person to talk to. . . .

At any rate, Bernstein, I felt, was looking in the wrong direction by trying to peer into the White House. I explained to him the nature of White House staffing, and that being a junior aide meant one never had a full picture of things, even if there were misdeeds. There was nothing I could do to help; I knew nothing.

Later, the questions would rise again. Was it possible something *was* going on all about me? And if so, why did I know nothing? Then came the most devastating question of my life to that point. As it became clear that some very sinister things had happened and that people in the White House had been at the center of activity, it hit me: Given your inexperience, political naiveté, ambition, awe, loss of critical objectivity, is it possible the only reason you're not involved is that you simply were not *asked?*

I wanted desperately to spin off that question—to cry out, "Nonsense!"—to piously assert that I was a perpetual Mr. Clean. But I began to see how I had succumbed to the Warp, how passionately I wanted to be Superaide. But I knew I couldn't. The whole process of introspection had shaken me to my boots. I had taken a hard look at me and was fast deciding

I didn't like what I was becoming. I had to leave the White House—maybe even get out of Washington altogether!

It was just about then all my efforts to land a continuing spot in government began to pay off. Four job possibilities opened up, at least three of them paying considerably more than what I was making at the White House. Just as I thought I had my decision and my integrity all wrapped up in a neat box, the job offers unravelled the whole package. That necessitated the raising of more painful questions and perceptions.

To really tangle up things, my old nemesis, the church, was back. Through the faithful persistence of my wife, we had maintained a semblance of church life during the Washington years. Before going into the White House, I had even been an interim pastor for a church in Maryland. But after joining the Presidential staff, my church life began to slide. I was involved with the prayer-fellowship movement in government, and found that greatly satisfying. But the church seemed to nag and bite at me.

We had joined a dynamic Virginia congregation, with a bold, aggressive ministry. The pastor was an outgoing Texan named Neal Jones. He and I became friends the moment we met. Occasionally, Neal would have lunch with me at the White House. We would talk, and in those rare objective moments, I would see I was far more excited about what he was doing than about my work as a staff assistant at the White House! That didn't compute, and I wouldn't let the thought linger in my mind. But it was so terribly annoying. The image of the pastorate in the minds of my colleagues who thought about it at all, surely was one of dullness and irrelevancy. Yet there I would sit, in unguarded moments envious of Neal, thinking how much he was at the center of action! I would conceive of myself as dealing with abstractions of politics and paper. He was dealing with people— walking, breathing people. I'm sure my frustration at not finding fulfillment in the White House caused me to underestimate the value and meaning of my own work, but I kept thinking: "Neal's much more 'where it's at' than I."

Ever since leaving the preaching ministry, I had had problems sitting in a church service. I rarely enjoyed the sermon, seldom felt blessed. The problem wasn't with the preachers—I had sat under the best. The problem was with me. Down at the deepest level of my spirit, I knew I ought to be serving somewhere. But even in those days when I was struggling with whether or not I ought to stay in Washington, I just couldn't admit that to myself.

As I battered through the decision some other troublesome feelings were cropping up. For one thing, I had taken a hard look at myself, and didn't like what I was becoming. I knew not everyone who worked in Washington was bent out of shape by its subtle forces. Yet, despite years of college and seminary and sermon-listening, I still had no cogent theology of power. Sometimes, I simply let myself flow in its path. After leaving the White House, I would probe all the areas of personal theology which my years in Washington had demonstrated were lacking in my life, and the result would be my first book *Enter at Your Own Risk*. But now, I was awash in ambiguity, sensing things were not right, but unable to put together the pieces.

As I understand it now, my religion then was idolatrous. I was like the Athenians Paul encountered who had a god on every street corner—a deity in every port. The gods I worshiped were far more subtle than golden calves and empty-hearted statues. But I believed and preached that whatever claimed a person's real commitment was his god. And I was certain of the things I would *not* do if the real God ordered me to do them. The lines were not as clear when it came to the commands of the gods of prestige and image I worshiped. I knew I would stop at clear illegality. My political ethic may have been infantile, but I did have one, going something like this: In a political campaign, issues are to be attacked, not persons. Yet . . . yet there was that lingering awareness that my commitment to the idols was deeper than that to the real God. Just how long would I have to remain in Washington before that ill-placed commitment would drive me to serious compromise and error?

The heady feel of the disease of *hubris* had set in. The symptoms of the ailment are very much like those of dying by suffocation. As death approaches, a light, gay giddiness overtakes the victim. He feels grandly assured that all is well just before death gobbles him up. If he is a diver starved of oxygen, he may cavort like a festive porpoise until that final shiver of death. Occasionally, a victim is fortunate, and someone gives him a hefty sniff of oxygen. Reality returns; death is averted. The return of my critical spirit was the fine rush of oxygen. It told me that the feeling that I was indestructible was not valid, and that if I did not surface soon, I would be lost forever!

7

Farewell to Foggy Bottom

So there I was at the bottom of Lake Quandary. I knew I had to leave government—maybe even depart Washington altogether. But where would I go? What would I do? That awful feeling of being a man without an identity was sinking over me again, as it had just after I had cut loose from the ministry. But someone had plunged into Lake Quandary and was getting ready to try to pull me to the surface.

During my years in Washington, Vincent Townsend, Sr., vice-president of the Birmingham *News,* and I had kept in touch. Our friendship was one of those highly unlikely ones. Townsend was pushing seventy; I was barely thirty. He was the typical newspaper executive: gruff, driving. When I first began work at the *News* in 1968, Townsend frightened me. I was religion editor, and had the distinct idea Townsend had as much use for religion as Genghis Khan had for lace doilies.

But there was something about Townsend I admired. At first, it was an intangible. But in the years we worked together, it shaped out. For one thing, no one I had ever known—except for my own wife—had the dogged determination of Vincent Townsend. A sign sat on his desk, reading: IF ALL POSSIBLE OB-

JECTIONS MUST FIRST BE OVERCOME, NOTHING WILL
EVER BE ACCOMPLISHED. And Townsend lived by
that credo.

The city of Birmingham had been written off by
many people when I first came to know Townsend.
Its racial antipathies and struggles had cut deeply
into the city's morale. But Vincent Townsend never
stopped believing in Birmingham's reconstruction.
He pushed and shoved and stepped on toes to the
extent his life was threatened. He felt deeply that
black and white people in Birmingham would have to
communicate with one another if there were to be a
restoration of peace. So he began organizing groups,
getting people talking.

Townsend himself came from a generation having
heavy ideological baggage on the race question. He
had all the marks of a southern aristocrat. He was
accused of changing for the wrong motives. But
wrong or right, I sensed Townsend had plowed
through some tempestuous change in his life, and I
admired him for taking the journey. He was loved or
hated; there was rarely middle ground in attitudes
about Townsend. Mayors quaked, white conservatives called him a "nigger lover," black militants labeled him a reactionary honkie, but they worked
with him, and the whole city was better for it.

While I loved my work at the *News,* my deepest
regret at having to leave there to go to Washington
was that I would have to tell Townsend I was resign-
ing.

Now it was nearly three years later, and my telephone was ringing—and it was Vincent Townsend.
He had read how the White House staff had been
ordered to prepare to resign. The *News,* he said,

would be willing to consider letting me return, if I wished. At first, I dismissed the offer. Again, my ego got in the way. The money would be sharply reduced from what I was getting and had been offered. And the *News* certainly wouldn't chauffeur me around in a big black car.

But on the other hand, I had enjoyed my work at the newspaper the first time. And now I might be able to make for myself a broader role. Maybe, I thought, I might even work into an executive spot. Then there might be the opportunity of developing a firecracker political column. Perhaps even some day I could return to Washington as a political journalist. For a man without a niche, that seemed a pretty fair one. I called Townsend.

Several days later, I flew to Birmingham, met with the *News* management and wrapped up the details. I would join the *News* as general affairs editor. None of us were certain what that meant, although we did talk about some political writing and administrative chores. Other responsibilities, we were certain, would evolve.

While Irene and I felt some relief from escaping the pressures of White House life, there would be some hard adjustments to make in the move to Birmingham. The hardest was in giving up our home, which we had decided was our residential resting place. It was agonizing realizing our geographical home and my professional home would not be in the same locality.

When we first moved to Washington, we had rented a townhouse in Virginia. Gradually, we came to despise the house. The rent was atrocious, and the basement-den flooded every time it rained, even though the place was brand new. Travis, then three, kept asking his mother, "When will we move out of this motel with a kitchen?"

We were reluctant to think of buying or building a home, since we had no idea what our future would be in Washington. But we scoured the area nevertheless. And one day Irene found it: A beautiful new subdivision had opened in Fairfax County, Virginia. I fell for the place as hard as did Irene. But, I told her, it would be foolish to buy a lot there and think of constructing a house.

One fall afternoon, however, I had been playing golf near the new subdivision. On the way home, I turned in, and cruised around some of the vacant lots. I spotted one with a slight uphill slope. I could picture a neocolonial home sitting on that very chunk of ground. I decided to simply inquire about the lot, but before I had left, I had given the realtor a check for earnest money on the property. Irene responded to my "surprise" as I had hoped. Though it was dark by the time I got to the townhouse, she insisted we ride out to the lot.

For nine months we rode back and forth to that site. Construction had begun on our new home as winter was setting in. Rains turned to snow and mud. But Saturday after Saturday, we would inspect the progress, counting every brick, perusing every new dig. The weather slowed construction, but finally the house was completed and we moved in. In mere days we knew we had found our resting place, and I could not conceive of leaving.

Now, only nine months after moving in, that's exactly what we were preparing to do! Early on a Sat-

urday morning , we placed a FOR SALE sign in front
of our home, and by that night we had sold it.

As the time for the move approached, we joked
about its rounding out our moves to an even dozen.
But I assured Irene that journalism was where my
heart was, and that she need not worry about having
to pull up stakes again. The transition would be an
easy one. And despite the pain at leaving our new
home, a good job awaited me, our families were in
Birmingham. We could make a good life there.

As we were packing two days before the move,
Irene's sister called from Birmingham. Their father
had been critically injured in an automobile accident.
It did not appear he would die, but we knew we
should hasten. The trip, made in two cars through
snow, took two days. We arrived in Birmingham on
Sunday afternoon, and went to the hospital as rapidly
as we could. We were not prepared for the extent of
his injuries. Miraculously, he pulled through the accident, and a year later was on his feet.

A week after returning to Birmingham, I was back
at work at the *News*. My reintroduction to the paper's readers was a series on my White House experiences. But the thing was too close, and I couldn't
really relate my feelings. Often, I sat at my desk, reflecting on the fact I was right back where I had
been three years before. It was as if I had simply
been gone on an expedition for a few days.

Something was definitely missing. I seemed to
have to struggle to produce a newspaper column.
During my first period at the *News*, I had developed
friendships with the people on the staff I really enjoyed. Taking and dishing out kidding has always
been part of my makeup. When I was religion editor,

some of my colleagues called me the "Bishop." That meant a lot; to me, it demonstrated their acceptance of me, and I wanted that badly. But now it all gnawed at me. I couldn't sit in an editorial staff meeting and discuss issues without crumbling into anger and frustration. I bawled out so many people, it was a wonder I had any friends left. Instead of a bright, cheery optimist, I was a bent and irritable old man.

Prior to leaving Washington, we had discovered Irene would need surgery. The weeks of her recuperation seemed to plod through a soggy spring. Lauri, our daughter, was now in her third school *that year*. At each, the work had been at a different level. Now she struggled to catch up with the new class, while trying to make adjustments to new people. Through her own persistence, the grace of a thoroughly Christian teacher, and our burning midnight oil at the kitchen table, Lauri did well. I had never been so proud of her. But the adjustment was not the easy thing I had thought it would be. There were times we wondered if we would make it.

My spirit was broken in a way it had never been before. In all the other times, I had been able to grasp the hand of God and let Him tug me out of the slough. In those times, there had been a future. Now God was done with me, and I with Him. And as far as I could see it, there was no future. *At age thirty-one, my life was over!*

Colonel Edwin "Buzz" Aldrin, one of the astronauts on the first moon landing, wrote one of the most poignant books I have ever read. In it, he recounted his efforts to readjust to life after achieving the goal of walking on the moon. His book is entitled (aptly) *Return to Earth* (New York: Random House). He candidly talks about the agony of mental depression brought about by the realization his greatest goal was behind him. Aldrin says he became limp professionally, suffering from something the psychiatrists call "dysfunction." He had no interest in his jobs during the deep despondency. And I thought of the days I sat at the *News* not caring whether words spilled out on my typewriter or not. I had not been to the moon but I *had* been to the White House.

Often while there, I met people for whom a post at the White House had been their crowning achievement, the summation or apex of their life's work. The question always lingered in my mind: *Where do you go from the White House?* As far as I was concerned in those horrid days of readjustment I was thirty-one years old and already had been at the top. The rest of my life would be a holding pattern between boredom and death. There was no place else to go!

Investigative assignments took me back to Washington. It only deepened my malaise to have to get security clearance at the gate of the White House to get to a friend's office. The newspaper work was interesting enough, though. Other trips took me to New Orleans, Los Angeles. I organized an investigative team and probed Alabama government. We did a major history of the racial changes in Birmingham over the decade 1963–1973. Some of the work would win awards. But for all that, I was still empty.

Irene had begun to sense it. We were both crushed. I thought seriously about going through psychoanalysis. Someday, I thought, I've *got* to be satisfied with what I'm doing.

Mixed with that biting frustration was the growing

awareness of the Watergate affair. My desk at the newspaper was near the wire machines, and daily—hourly—they would clatter out new revelations about people I knew. Bob Mardian, my first boss in Washington, was being indicted in the cover-up. Names of other people I had known seemed to pour out of the machines. The faces of these people were etched on television tubes all around me.

One of those faces I don't remember seeing until I watched it on television. It was that of John W. Dean III. He had occupied an office at the other end of the Executive Office Building from our suite, and I didn't even know what Dean looked like. Once, before leaving the White House, I had heard a senior official speculating on the mess. His idea was that if the involvement were close to the President, the guilty might try to find others in the White House on whom to shift the blame. I didn't know if the man was serious or not. But early in John Dean's testimony before the Watergate committee, I couldn't help but wonder if he were part of some sinister plot to focus blame away from those near the President. Our office had not fared well with the White House hierarchy, as I understood it. My balance and perspective already eroded, the chilling question entered my mind: Will someone attempt to bring me into this thing?

I probably flattered myself by assuming that any of the White House powers even remembered I had been there. I had been one of a hundred faceless mechanics dashing through the corridors. And I knew that any effort to tie me to the Watergate would have to be concocted from nothing. But my basic insecurity intensified. Was this a political vendetta? Had

Nixon's opponents determined that the more of his aides they could discredit, the more criminal he would look? Were his closest aides now convinced that the way to save themselves and possibly the President (I still was convinced he had nothing to worry about, personally; I wasn't to change my mind on that until I read the tape transcripts) was to let everyone else "twist slowly in the wind"?

Finally, one afternoon in May, 1973, I had all I could take. The televised Watergate hearings blared out on our newsroom monitor, the wire machines beat out a hysterical death march. I had to get out of the atmosphere of the place. So I left the office, went to my car, and started driving. And it was a while before I realized I was praying. I'm not sure what I said in the prayers, except they came from a spirit in which I had never before prayed. Always before, my prayers had gone up on a cloud of arrogant conceit through which I subconsciously thought that God was actually quite lucky to have me on His side. Now the words stirred from a broken, crushed spirit. All my idols were caving in—the human messianism, the religion of power and prestige, the sanctity of image to which I had given myself. My gods were dying and I was horribly frightened. Maybe the prayers were of a foxhole variety. But this is the marvel of grace: God observes our spiritual adultery against Him, but in that inevitable moment when we try to climb back, He says, "I forgive you. . . ."

Now, as I prayed, a response seemed to be shaping in my mind. Words seemed to appear. They said: "You've fooled around long enough. You've been proud of your ability to pull strings for yourself.

You've maneuvered yourself to the edge of the abyss. Now, go serve Me!"

By my theology, one didn't get such direct communications from God. My religion to that point was largely a philosophical one knowing little about the experiential side of faith. That was for Moses and Abraham and the apostles. It was reserved for a different period of history. Sometime during my college days, I had decided it was impossible to have a clear grasp of the specifics of God's will for a person. I felt the best one could do was say a prayer, then do what he wanted to do, hoping it was right. That was why it had been so easy to twist my calling in the first place.

Irene had never felt that way. She had always believed devoutly that God led her in specific ways, and had tried to warn me. At first, I kept from her my new feelings about reentering the ministry. We had only been in our "permanent" home in Birmingham less than six months. She was recuperating from surgery, and still going through an agonizing vigil with her father. I just couldn't tell her I was thinking of moving again.

But I had to. So one summer afternoon, I laid out the whole story. It had been weeks since I felt the impression to get into the ministry, and the desire was not fading—it was growing. Whatever doubts I had about what I ought to do were fading. So I said, "Honey, I don't know how or where, but it looks like we're going to have to make another transition." Then I explained what had been happening inside me. When I was finished, she replied, "I won't go along with it." My countenance plunged into the Grand Canyon. But she finished her statement. "I won't simply go along with it, I demand it! I've been married to you twelve years, and I've known all those years what's wrong with you. God called you long ago to preach."

For the first time, I realized what Irene had been through. For a dozen years, she had been willing to jump all over the place, from one so-called green field to another, knowing each time that only more emptiness and spiritual desolation and another move would follow. She had tried before to tell me what was wrong, but I had never listened. Nevertheless, she had always been there when my worlds came tumbling in. And each time, she would muffle her own pain to bind me up and give me the legs to walk on again. And I understood as never before the beauty of our kind of marriage.

In the months that followed, I could feel something good happening inside me. I no longer had to wear a face. I was free from pretense. A new level of openness to God had been forced on my spirit. Like C. S. Lewis, I had been tugged to this kicking and fighting, but it was a discovery of the deepest joy. I felt like a leaf being carried on a firm but gentle wind, not like a twig snapping under the onslaught of a tornado. The incredible thing was that this basic joy existed midst the fear that still plagued my mind. But I was coming to understand the more of myself I released to Christ, the less the fear would grip me. It would be almost two years before the full meaning of that would hit me, but it was growing.

I began to share with close friends what was happening to me spiritually. Some of them had been the targets of my most biting columns as a religion editor, years before. I knew a little of what Paul must have felt like when, after his conversion, he began relating to those he had once hoped to finish off. My friends *were friends!* They prayed with, accepted me.

But the best thing that happened was the restoration of my future! And the present, existential joy had been thrown in as an extra. That old feeling that my life was over was replaced with the thrill of anticipation over the future. I saw myself on the threshold of adventure. I was embarking on an exploration of the outer limits of the universe; all the probing under my own steam had been mere excursions down the street!

And on November 4, 1973, after a process it would require another book to detail, I found myself pastor of a small Baptist church near Mobile, Alabama. I knew from the moment of my first sermon at Old Spanish Fort Baptist Church that I did not want to swap that pulpit for all the desks in the White House, where I'd been just one year before.

8

Up From the White House

One morning in the fall of 1974, Bob Curlee and I were driving from Mobile up to Maxwell Air Force Base, to visit Chuck Colson at the Federal Prison Camp there. Bob had every right to be a first-class grump that day. He edges slightly over six feet tall, and I had him crammed in my tiny two-passenger sports car. His knees kneaded his Adam's apple, and it would be so for the 150 miles we had to travel.

Despite that, Bob was very nice. "I used to have a hard time reading your newspaper columns," he said. "Before all this business with the White House, there seemed little kindness in what you wrote. Now I detect a willingness to be more fair with people."

I really had not been aware of any great change in my journalistic style. But I did perceive some conceptual changes. In the earlier period Bob had been referring to, I had been very much the new-generation journalist. Situations were seen as black or white; people did wrong things because they were all bad; and they did good things because they were all good. There were no grays—no room for genuine struggle.

That philosophy, pitted with the bitterness left over from my childhood and the frustration of my own soul of not doing the will of God, sparked some of the most vicious newspaper columns to leap from a typewriter. As a religion editor, I measured my success on the number of preachers and denominational executives I was at war with at a given time. It's not that I was always wrong and they were invariably right; it's just that wrong or right, I went after scalps with a vengeance!

Now Bob said I had changed. Perhaps it was because, as a government official, I had been up against some of the very same kind of reporters I had been. Maybe it was because I had known men in the White House and other branches of government who were downright good people, but who had been cast as the lowest criminals. But as Bob talked that morning, I hoped the change was more fundamental than that. My prayer was (and is) that any change in the way I write about people reflecting a more generous spirit toward their motives, comes from the work of the Holy Spirit.

I still believe in aggressive journalism, but I am appalled at the zeal I had at slashing up people with newspaper copy. In the months I was trying to develop a column at the *News,* on my return there from Washington, it occurred to me that I may have succumbed to the notion that my success as a probing newspaperman might be in proportion to just how skillful I was in destroying people. In my opinion, one of the best columns I had done from the point of view of that school of journalism, had been a burning attack on one of Alabama's officials. My point was that I felt he was trying to use state money to build his political organization. But I didn't write about the inadequacy of the political system nearly as much as

I did that man. Later, the column would cause me to want to burn it. The more I thought about it, the more I realized that if this was success in journalism, I wanted nothing of it.

Obviously, not ever journalist is so motivated. Nor is every incisive piece of investigative and revealing reporting drummed up from such a nasty backdrop of attitudes. But for me in those times, I saw a penchant to transfer my hurt to somebody else, via newspaper columns.

If my style of writing about people had changed, it was simply indicative of a whole series of little revolutions exploding all over me. In the crucible of history, I had come up against God in a radical way I never had before, and His truth would not let me rest. Now I understood more clearly Jacob's wrestling match with God out at Brook Jabbok. And there was Saul of Tarsus, beating his brains out to get some success in life, but getting nowhere until God zapped him blind on dusty Damascus Road. The gurgling of Brook Jabbok could be heard that long night with human ears; a man's mouth could taste the real dust of the Damascus Road on Saul's day of revolution. The struggles between a person and God don't happen between an invisible spirit and a divine whisper in a dark notch of the universe; they happen in rooms clouded with cigar smoke and greasy with the oil of rustling machines. As Francis Schaeffer says again and again, God is *there,* and we struggle with Him in the *there* of our existential moments. And we never emerge the same.

The starkest level of this struggle with God and me went on over my incessant fear. Poor Irene had such a hard time listening to my sermons on faith, then watching me crumble up in fear at the slightest *boo*. Something had to be done about it, if I were to be a credible servant of God, to say nothing of my personal faith.

One of my first undertakings at the White House was to keep up with Governor George Wallace and do periodic analysis of his political standing. I thought nothing sinister of that task when I was given it in 1971. My boss, Harry Dent, according to the press and everybody else who knew the White House structure, was Nixon's prime advisor on southern politics. Governor Wallace was the South's major political figure. The Presidency of the United States was a political office, and its holder ought to know something about his potential challengers, so I thought nothing strange about the assignment to do analysis on the political strength of the governor. I had done it often as a newspaper columnist.

Also, whenever the President traveled, it was our job to prepare him a briefing on the area he was going into, and the people who would host him. It was not our desire to dig up dirt on these people, but to let the President know their stance on issues he might be discussing with them, and personal tidbits he might want to raise in conversation to add humanity to the meeting. Since I prepared most of these briefings, I tried to know as much as I could about many leaders in areas Nixon visited.

So, when he journeyed to Alabama, I prepared a paper on Governor Wallace. Nixon, I had been told, wanted to avoid conversation about politics while he and Wallace would be together, so I inserted in the briefing some interesting hobbies of the new Mrs. Wallace—like water skiing and automobile racing.

My method of getting information was through major regional newspapers. Dent was already subscribing to the big Alabama dailies when I went to work there, and they covered Wallace quite extensively. Also, I would converse periodically with friends in Alabama who kept abreast of the political situation. I would then try to analyze what all the information meant. Using so-called spies to gather information or do political espionage never entered my mind. In retrospect, I'm grateful I did not know that others were allegedly using such techniques. My passion to be Superaide might have caused me to abandon caution.

The only contact I had with anyone during that period was with Wallace's former national campaign manager, Tom Turnipseed. Turnipseed had been fired or had resigned from his job with Wallace—I never understood which. He and Dent were both from South Carolina, and had known each other previously, as I understood it. Turnipseed occasionally called Dent, and there were a few times Dent asked me to take the call, as I did with many people who called our office. At any rate, I don't remember talking with Turnipseed more than three times. The calls were always incidental, but I'm sure I probably picked Turnipseed's brain from time to time on what this or that meant in terms of Wallace's possible campaign. Some of that may have wound up in my analysis memoranda to Dent (which I discovered one day he was forwarding to Bob Haldeman and others).

It would be absurd for me to say I had no political interest in all this. At the time, I was a Nixon partisan, and I believed a Wallace candidacy would do harm to Nixon in the South, and said so frequently. The number of other political observers who also held that view almost made the point moot. So I went happily along in my work, feeling I was making a real contribution to the fortunes of the President of the United States.

Months later, I would hear and read the tales of political espionage and "dirty tricks" being committed in the Watergate period. Day after day, I would be tortured with the wonder of whether or not my bits and pieces of analysis had been used, without my knowledge, in some broader political operations, although I could not imagine how. The worries deepened my fear in a way I had never known before. My stomach went in rebellion, and I was sick for weeks on end. The tension caused serious hyperventilation, and at times I would have to struggle for air. I could not sleep at night. To my family, I became remote, insensitive. The toll of fear was destroying me physically and emotionally.

I reached the bottom of the valley of fear on the weekend of July 12, 1974. On Friday night, a reporter called to get my reaction to a story his newspaper was carrying the next morning. According to the article, the House Judiciary Committee, then deliberating the impeachment of Nixon, had a memorandum in which Gordon Strachan told his boss, Bob Haldeman, that I was monitoring Governor Wallace through Turnipseed.

I fought panic. I told the reporter that I monitored the Wallace political effort, but that no spying or proposals for "dirty tricks" had ever been involved. I hung up from the conversation facing more of those gnawing, frightening questions. I knew I had told the truth, but in the Watergate atmosphere, who would believe me? I had found great happiness and fulfillment as a preacher, but what would all this do to my congregation, to my own credibility as a minister of the Gospel? Was I now being destroyed?

I telephoned Don Conlon, chairman of the deacons at Old Spanish Fort Baptist Church. "I've got to talk with you right away," I said. Soon, Don, and his wife, Karen, were sitting in our den. I told them the whole story, and that I expected the newspapers to break it that weekend. "I don't know where all this is going, and I can't stand the thought of embarrassing the church," I said. "So, I am prepared to offer my resignation this Sunday."

Don had seen one of his jobs as chairman of the deacons to be that of ministering to me when I was in need. Now, he measured to the best of that task. "Pastor, you're overreacting, and besides, I know our people and I know they will want to stand with you no matter what," he replied.

That night, after the conversation with Don, I was at least able to sleep a little. But I still dreaded the newspaper headlines I knew would flash the following morning, Saturday. Only the paper which had first discovered the story carried it that Saturday morning. But throughout that day I fretted, knowing the wire services would have the piece all over the state by Sunday. And it was dawning on me that many of my people would come to church Sunday morning after having read that their pastor seemed to be a political spy! I knew I would have to be ready to say something. But what would it be?

Edith Schaeffer has written in her book *L'Abri* that there are days whose events are so significant they should be heralded with trumpet blasts, signs, signals. Had there been such symbols of the significance of that day, they would have been funeral marches if they were to match my spirit. But there were no signals, and so my people continued to see me as pastor, not as alleged political spy. And a family needed me that evening. I had already set up the appointment. Several times, I started to cancel the meeting. I could not minister to people when I was falling apart myself, I thought. But no, I realized my work as a pastor had to go on.

As I dressed that Saturday afternoon to go to the family's home, it became clear I could stand no more. I would be unable to help the people I was on my way to see; and the next morning I would have to stand in my pulpit and say some words about faith and hope. I would either have to flee those responsibilities, or have my own spirit changed, otherwise it would all be a farce—hypocrisy of the worst order!

So I picked up my phone and dialed one of the fiercest prayer warriors I had ever known. I let her in on my horrible secret. "What I have now is the spirit of fear," I told her, "and I know that's not pleasing to God. But there's no way I can minister in His name when I'm dying of fright." She began to pray, right there on the telephone. "God, liberate Wally from this tonight," she begged.

Releasing burdens to God is very much like releasing the energy of an atom. Very often, in the case of the burdens—always, in the case of the atom—a triggering device is needed. My friend's prayer bombarded my cringing soul as infinitesimal particles crashing into an atom's nucleus. As she prayed, I felt a transferrence of my fear, I sensed it flowing outward from me into God.

The flowing out takes time. It would be many months before I really felt I was on top of that fear. But that night I was ecstatic. Something wonderful had begun in me. I went home, talked long into the night with the family. Even later that evening, I was summoned to the hospital to the bedside of a man suffering from heart attack. I stayed until the wee hours of Sunday morning. But still I felt fear was on the run. I felt confident about Sunday, that I would know precisely what to say to my congregation.

Just as expected, the Sunday newspaper in our city carried, on page one, the story saying that a local pastor denied being a political spy. The article, I thought, was well done, and quoted me accurately. Before I left for church, Don, remembering how distraught I had been on Friday night, called to see how I was doing, "Great!" I replied. And I meant it.

While I had been deep in fear's canyon on Saturday, I had drafted a twelve-page statement I was going to read to the church. But now, on Sunday morning, as I arrived at my office, I knew I didn't need that document. I sensed so strongly the Lord would tell me what to say. And that morning, as I rose to preach, the words shaped out like this:

You probably read my name in the newspaper this morning. You may read it again. I do not know what the future holds. I do know that I have never willfully committed a crime in my life. But I also know I was in the White House during a tragic period.

MENTIONED IN REPORT

No 'spying,' former
White House aide says

BY AL FOX
News staff writer

The latest name to make the news in the Watergate hearings is that of a former Birmingham newsman and a one-time White House staff member who served in President Richard Nixon's political liaison office.

He is Wallace Henley, former religion editor of The Birmingham News who is now pastor of a Baptist church in Spanish Fort. Henley served for almost three years as an aide to Harry Dent of South Carolina who directed the political liaison office in the first Nixon administration.

Henley's name came into the news when evidence presented to the House Judiciary Committee contained a memorandum from Gordon Strachan to H. R. "Bob" Haldeman, Nixon's chief advisor, which said that "Wallace Henley monitors George Wallace for Harry Dent through Tom Turnipseed, Wallace's former campaign manager."

HENLEY TOLD The News that "there was no political espionage or spying" within the duties or responsibilities of his assignment.

"I never met Turnipseed to my knowledge," Henley said, "and talked to him on the telephone on three occasions as I recall when Dent was not available."

Turnipseed, former national director of the Wallace organization returned to his native South Carolina after Wallace's third party effort in 1968 and is

Turnipseed were acquaintances prior to both becoming involved in national politics and he knew they talked on occasions after Turnipseed left the official Wallace organization.

Henley was one of three aides to Dent who were assigned different regions to keep in touch with the political pulse in preparation for Nixon's bid for a second term in the White House.

"I kept Dent aware of the Wallace situation in the South, his position on various issues and his response to administration positions. It was an evaluation of how Gov. Wallace, as either a Democratic or third-party candidate, would affect the President's campaign," Henley said.

"It was our opinion that Wallace held a balance of power and we were to prepare an analysis of his political strength from newspaper reports, talks with reporters, political figures and others close to issues," he said.

"It was the type of research conducted by all major political candidates," Henley said. "There was no underground type operation to it."

HE POINTED out that when President Nixon visited Mobile and Wallace flew from the port city to Birmingham with him on then Air Force One, he prepared what was referred to as a "talk plan" for the President. "It was a briefing on issues and non-controversial items in which Gov. Wallace had an interest and would give an op-

now a candidate for the Democratic nomination for attorney general in South Carolina.

Henley said that Dent and portunity for small talk during the flight if the President didn't want to talk about other matters."

Reprinted from the Birmingham *News*, Sun., July 14, 1974.

In counseling sessions, I have told many of you to rejoice in times of stress, and let God be the Lord of your suffering. I have urged you to praise Him for all things, in the confidence that He loves you and is working all things toward good for them who love Him and are called by Him.

Now it is time for me to show you that I really mean it when I tell you that. If I fail in this time of severe testing, you have every right never to believe me again. But I pledge to you and to my family, that through Him, I will not fail. . . .

All day that Sunday, I was captivated by what I can only describe as exhilaration. Certainly, I would slip and slide into the valley again, but now I had been to the top of the mountain, and the valley would never again be enshrouded in hopelessness! At that point, I caught myself praying a prayer that, upon reflection, caused me to tremble a little: "Lord, if people know I am under intense pressure, and they see me bear this with grace in Your power, Your name will be glorified, so pour on grace and tribulation, if You wish. . . ."

As I say, later I would wonder if I ought to retract that prayer. My joy that Sunday was so full, things like that were just popping out. But my liberation had happened at a much deeper level too, and I couldn't take back those words. I began to see that perhaps all this business with fear had brought me to the desperation that can drive a person's life to the openness to God required if one is really to be His servant. And I really understood for the first time that God would not put on me more than His grace could cover.

The most precious lesson coming from this experience was the experiential knowledge that God is in full charge of the futures of His children. I say it was *experiential knowledge,* because it was a stark contrast to what I had known before. The providence of God for His people was something I had believed and preached. But now it was mine by *experience,* and there is vast difference in believing something with the intellect and experiencing it existentially. I don't know how else to say it: For the first time, I *experienced* the providence of God!

Precepts so simple they staggered me were lodging in my mind. Now I saw that I was to let God be Lord of my life in the same sense that He is Lord of the sun and moon, in terms of control. I did not lie awake nights worrying about their comings and goings, because I knew He was in charge. I knew that I was *person,* not a heavenly body, and if He controlled them, He could certainly control me! At last I understood what Jesus meant when He talked about God caring for the lilies of the field. The focus of that passage was not the lilies, but people, who are far more precious to the Father than flowers.

So Francis Schaeffer was right when he suggested that to be embroiled in discontent is to deny the Lordship of Christ over one's life. In those moments when fear would attempt to creep back in, spiritual discipline was called for, in the form of *practicing* this control of God. Over and over I would say to myself, "God is in charge of my future, God is in charge of my future. . . ." I would repeat that until fear's loud taunts were stifled by the trumpet of that assurance. And it was not an assurance based on escape, or a flimsy notion that because I was in Christ I would never again confront tribulation. It was much better than that. It was the experiential knowledge that in the midst of whatever happened in my future, He would be with me there, guiding, controlling.

Months later, the works of Watchman Nee, the valiant Chinese Christian, would have deep impact on my life. There was such an existential reality to Nee's faith! Much of his writing is concerned with the inner person, controlled by God's Spirit, breaking through the natural person. Watchman Nee talks of rigorous discipline, of God's sparking His fires in the life of the believer so that the chaff is burned away. Then Nee himself faces the challenge of remaining in Shanghai to minister when to do so will mean persecution and imprisonment. Nee stays, and winds up jailed for twenty years—until his death.

In his book *Changed Into His Likeness*, Watchman Nee talks of Jacob. And he says that Jacob's problem was not that he didn't want to do the will of God. His problem was that he wanted to fulfill that will in his own way, on his own terms. But, says Nee, ". . . God must bring us to the place of weakness, the place where we cannot think or plan or do apart from Him."

And in that long, bloody climb up from the White House, it was now coming home to me so clearly: *You don't have to maneuver yourself anymore; the only requirement is that you be open to God, and to His way!*

I perused the years past. I knew they had consisted of one game after another, all part of the scheme by which I worked my way into doing what I hoped, secondarily, to be the will of God. But now it was so utterly, utterly simple. He knew the *eschaton*, the end, the goal, and He knew the route. My job was not to build my own train, but to hop on His.

Irene and I had often laughed about my penchant to "Keep all my options open." I worked arduously to cultivate the people I thought I would need later to help me maneuver myself. That in itself was antichristian, in that I reduced so many people to mere instruments. They were nothing more than pitons for me to grasp on my climb up Success Mountain! Such an objectifying use of human beings for whom Christ died is the essence of obscenity.

Words are far too limited to convey the radical liberation this new understanding brought my spirit. Now I was free from the corrupting shackles of having to weigh my relationships with people on the scales of how they could help me get to my destination. I was unbound from the necessity of viewing every circumstance from the perspective of how I could manipulate it for my own ends. God was in charge of that. My only assignment was to be open to Him and to people, in His Spirit!

To this point, I had been the deckhand, cranking a hand-driven generator which fed oxygen to a diver at the bottom of the sea. Only I had been the diver, too. I had wearied at turning that crank. At times, it seemed my arm would fall off. I wanted to stop, to sleep, to take food. But I knew if I did the diver would suffocate, he would lose his life. Then the liberation: God took the handle of the life-machine. I no longer had to pump. I was free to be the diver, and only had to breathe the air as He sent it to me. To learn that alone made the White House experience and all its pain worthwhile!

But I suppose the most important realization that came to me with this struggle with God in the crucible of history was the knowledge that a person is never fulfilled until he or she is doing God's perfect will. I had tried every way but His, had the things and situations that, by my prescription, should have brought me a sense of wholeness and purpose. But I had been empty until driven to submission to Him.

Ministering in the name of Christ had been an either/or proposition for me. Either one did his work of ministry in the secular world, or he did it in the church. At various stages of my life, one form had seemed wrong, the other right. Now I saw that God worked, not in broad generalities, but in specific categories. Further, each personality-type He designed was suited to a certain category of ministry. My friend Cal Thomas, the television commentator, was a minister because he had yielded his life to Christ. And so was my old classmate, Don Graves, who was pastor of a church. Each was finding fulfillment through submission to God's will. And that submission had been elevated to the stage of happy acceptance.

When my first book was published, I traveled to Shreveport, Louisiana, for some appearances. On the afternoon I was to fly home, a severe thunderstorm hit the Shreveport area. I'm a nervous flyer, and raging storms don't help. Nevertheless, hoping the weather would clear, I went to the airport. I sat in the waiting area, listening as it was announced that one flight after another was overflying Shreveport because of weather. I was really hoping my flight would do the same.

But I was not to be freed from that flight. A momentary break in the weather permitted the airplane to land. Questioning my sanity, which I shortly expected to lose, I climbed aboard. An aisle seat in the middle was available, but I spotted something more to my taste ahead. No sooner had I buckled myself in the seat than the stewardess informed me it was her chair, and that I would have to move.

So I returned to the aisle seat I had rejected seconds earlier. A young man sat by the window. After the airplane had taken off and finished its bucking, yawing dash to cruising altitude, I felt compelled to strike up conversation with him. As we talked, we exchanged bits of information on employment and family. Then I began to share with him some of the things in this book, especially the struggles I had gone through in a long rejection of God's will for my life. As I talked, he gazed out the window, his face turned away from me. But suddenly he turned it to me. He was weeping. "Why are you telling me all this?" he asked. "Why . . . because I felt compelled to," I answered.

Then he told me his story: God had called him to the ministry, and he had even spent a while in a Bible school. But several years earlier, he had spurned that call. For the first time, he was admitting that he had not had a moment's peace since turning off God. "Pray for me," he said, and we prayed at that moment. And when we finished, I could tell the young man had yielded his life in a new and deeper way. As we entered the approach pattern for New Orleans, he said, "I wish this flight would never end; I have never known such peace. . . ."

I knew how he felt. For there is no more stark conflict yet no more complete fulfillment than giving oneself unreservedly to God's specific purpose!

I have noticed in writing these past paragraphs that I have violated a cardinal principle of mine in writing. A writer should never overdo his exclamation points. When he does, he wastes them. They become routine, cheap. An exclamation point is like penicillin: Too much use can dilute effectiveness. Yet as I have written, they have been spontaneous. Many months have passed since my "rediscovery of Jesus"—to use Malcolm Muggeridge's wonderful idea. Yet I find the only way to convey my excitement and thrill and sense of adventure and fulfillment is an abundant use of exclamation points! *There.*

Ah, yes, there are many nights when I still wake up beside Brook Jabbok, wrestling and grappling to overcome fear, isolation feelings, self-sovereignty. The struggle is not done. But being in Christ brings beauty to the warfare. The struggle is my future in Him. And the beauty is that my partner in combat is God. And every time I lose and He wins, the most amazing paradox takes place: *I am the winner!*